COOKING
WITH **WILD BERRIES & FRUITS**
OF INDIANA, KENTUCKY AND OHIO

by Teresa Marrone

Adventure Publications, Inc.
Cambridge, MN

ACKNOWLEDGMENTS

Thanks to Lisa Schindler for information and help with muscadines. Also, a big thanks to Bruce Bohnenstingl for help with the wine recipe, and for being willing to eat the results of my recipe testing without complaint.

Cover and book design by Jonathan Norberg

Cover photo: Black raspberries by Cindy Seigle

Edited by Dan Downing

10 9 8 7 6 5 4 3 2 1

Copyright 2011 by Teresa Marrone
Published by Adventure Publications, Inc.
820 Cleveland Street South
Cambridge, Minnesota 55008
1-800-678-7006
www.adventurepublications.net

ISBN: 978-1-59193-308-3
also available in paper binding

TABLE OF CONTENTS

INTRODUCTION

Wild berries and fruits are everywhere, once you learn to look for them. You'll find raspberries growing in the shrubby areas around the playground, elderberries on the edges of cattail swamps, and blackhaws growing in forest remnants that have been kept as buffers around office parks. Some species, like blueberries, blackberries and raspberries, look just like commercially available fruits, although in the wild they are usually smaller. Others have never been commercialized, and so will be unfamiliar at first.

This book celebrates edible wild berries and fruits. It includes information and recipes for over 50 species that are found in our area. Here you'll find recipes for sauces, baked goods, and other foods made with these delicious wild fruits. (For more information on identifying these plants, please see the companion book, *Wild Berries & Fruits Field Guide of Indiana, Kentucky and Ohio.*)

One thing to keep in mind is that wild fruits are much less consistent than domestic fruits, which have been bred for specific flavor characteristics (as well as the ability to withstand the rigors of packing and shipping). When working with wild fruits, it may be necessary to adjust the amount of sugar, for example, if the fruit you've picked isn't as sweet as it might be. If you use wild fruits in recipes calling for the same type of domestic fruit, you may need to adjust quantities; wild fruits are typically smaller and pack more closely together, so a cup of wild blueberries weighs more than a cup of domestic blueberries.

Another very important thing to remember is that wild fruits have not been thoroughly tested for possible adverse reactions in sensitive individuals. Some foods—both wild and domestic—simply don't agree with everyone. When you're sampling a wild fruit for the first time, eat only a small portion to make sure that you won't have a problem.

It is also worth stressing that before eating something which you've harvested from the wild, you must be *absolutely certain* that the plant has been identified properly. Further, it's important to realize that even if the fruit of a plant is edible, the leaves and other parts may make you sick if you eat them. Some fruits are mildly toxic when underripe; others have pits or seeds that contain harmful substances, and so require specific preparation. This book attempts to alert the reader to possible problems, but it's still a good practice to get assistance from a knowledgeable forager before harvesting or preparing unfamiliar wild foods.

How This Book Is Organized

Fruits are listed in alphabetical order, by their common name. In several cases, similar fruits have been grouped because they are interchangeable in recipes; for example, blueberries and huckleberries are in one section.

Each species includes a bit of general information about the plant, including any harvesting tips that might be particularly helpful. If the fruit is commonly juiced, instructions are included with this general information. You'll learn how to successfully preserve your harvest by freezing, if appropriate. Recipes for each species are included; and at the end of each species, there's a list of recipes elsewhere in the book that use that particular fruit, as well as some quick ideas for using the fruit.

After the individual species, there are two recipes that use mixed fruits, as well as six recipes using juice or syrup from virtually any of the fruits in this book. Following this are instructions on how to make jelly and jam; each species includes measurements for making jelly and jam (when appropriate), but rather than repeating the same instructions multiple times, the specific instructions are written on pgs. 178–181. The book concludes with general information that pertains to many different fruits, such as instructions on dehydrating berries and fruits, making fruit leather, and instructions for sterilizing jars and canning.

You'll also find useful tips throughout the book. These explain things like how to make a lattice-top pie crust, zesting lemons and other citrus fruits, and how to make an improvised double boiler. These tips apply to a number of recipes in the book and will make cooking easier.

APPLES and CRABAPPLES *(Malus* spp.)

Apples aren't native to the United States, but they may be found in the wild in our area as escapees from cultivation, "planted" by birds or, perhaps, by a picnicker who casually discarded an apple core into the woods. You might also find apple trees that are remnants of an abandoned orchard, or those that still grow on old homestead sites. Typically, these feral apples are smaller than commercially grown varieties, and are often misshapen and blotchy. However, they are great for eating or cooking; simply cut away and discard any damaged or wormy portions.

Crabapples are found just about everywhere, from urban parks and forests, to abandoned fields, to shelterbelts and woodlots. Apples are less common in the wild; most are found in abandoned orchards or on old homesites.

Numerous varieties of crabapple grow in our region; some are native, but others are cultivated varieties that have escaped into the wild. Although size, shape and color vary dramatically, all are edible. Larger fruits, ¾ inch across or more, work best for making purée, or for cutting up to use in recipes; tiny crabapples have a lot of seeds in comparison to the amount of flesh, and it's next to impossible to remove the seeds without destroying the fruit. However, tiny crabapples can be used to make juice; the high proportion of skin makes the juice a particularly deep pink color. Large crabapples can be used to make juice also, but since they are more versatile, you may wish to save them for recipes that call for cut-up fruit.

Apples and crabapples, especially those that are slightly underripe, are rich in natural pectin; the juice can be used to make jelly without the commercial pectin needed for most jellies. Even though the juice may look a bit cloudy, the jelly will be clear as long as you don't squeeze the fruit during juicing.

To prepare apple or crabapple juice, cut fruits in half (or into quarters or eighths if large), removing stems and blossom ends; if fruit has soft spots or bugs, cut away and discard the affected portions. Place in non-aluminum pot; add water to cover the fruit completely. Heat to boiling over high heat. Reduce heat so mixture is simmering, then cover and simmer without stirring until the fruit is very soft, 20 to 25 minutes. Transfer the mixture to a strainer lined with doubled, dampened cheesecloth and let it drip for 30 minutes; if you're making jelly, don't squeeze the fruit or the jelly will be cloudy. After the liquid has dripped away, set it aside and squeeze the fruit into a different container; you can use this cloudy juice as a beverage or for cooking. Yield varies quite a bit, because apples and crabapples vary so much in size; in general, you'll get 2 cups of juice per pound of crabapples, or about 2½ cups per pound of apples.

If you have a fruit press, you can use it to make fresh apple cider from apples or crabapples. You may want to mix in some regular cider apples with the wild fruits, to balance the flavor. Home-pressed cider is a delicious beverage on its own, and can also be fermented to make an outstanding wine or hard apple cider. For more information on making apple wine or hard cider, consult a book on home winemaking such as *First Steps in Winemaking* by C.J.J. Berry or *The American Cider Book* by Vrest Orton.

Apple or Crabapple Jelly (no added pectin)
About 3 half-pints per 2 pounds of fruit

Crabapple or apple jelly has a pleasant flavor; if red-skinned crabapples are used, it will also have a lovely pink color.

Apple or crabapple juice

1 teaspoon lemon juice for each cup of juice

⅔ cup sugar for each cup of juice

Because this recipe does not use commercial pectin, it's more flexible; you can make as little as 2 pints, or as much as 5 pints, depending on how much fruit you've got. When preparing the juice, use a mix of ripe and slightly underripe fruit for the best flavor and texture. Please read "Jelly Instructions for Fruits with Natural Pectin" on pg. 180 to learn about testing for doneness.

Measure the juice; for each 2 cups of juice, prepare 3 half-pint canning jars, bands and new lids as directed on pg. 185. Place measured juice and lemon juice in a non-aluminum pot that holds at least four times the amount of juice you're using. For each cup of juice, measure ⅔ cup of sugar; set it aside. Heat juice to boiling over medium-high heat. Add sugar and cook, stirring constantly, until sugar dissolves. Increase heat to high and cook, skimming off any foam and stirring frequently, until jelly passes one or more of the doneness tests on pg. 180; this typically takes 10 to 15 minutes.

Once the jelly is done, skim any foam off the surface and pour the jelly, while still hot, into the prepared canning jars; seal with prepared lids and bands. Process in a water-bath canner (pg. 185) for 10 minutes, or store in the refrigerator.

Variation: Add a handful of fresh mint leaves to the crabapples when preparing the juice, for a delightful Crabapple- or Apple-Mint Jelly.

Make some extra jelly when apples or crabapples are in season, to use as holiday gifts. Cut a square of colorful fabric, large enough to cover the top of the canning jar; wrap it over the lid and tie in place with some pretty ribbon.

Crabapplejack

One fifth-sized bottle

Traditional applejack is a brandy that has been distilled from apple juice. Here's an easy way to make apple-flavored brandy.

2 cups small crabapples

1 fifth brandy

½ cup sugar, or to taste

You'll need a glass jar that holds at least 40 ounces, with a mouth wide enough to insert the crabapples; juice is often sold in these types of bottles. Wash it very well, then fill it with boiling water and let stand for at least 5 minutes.

Wash crabapples very well; remove stems and blossom ends. Drain water from bottle; add crabapples and brandy. Cap bottle, and place in a cupboard or other dark location that is room temperature or slightly cooler. Let steep for 8 to 10 weeks, gently shaking the bottle once or twice a week.

After the 8- to 10-week period, strain out and discard crabapples. Filter the brandy through a funnel lined with a paper coffee filter into a clean bottle; add sugar. Return the bottle to the cupboard, and let mellow for a few weeks before serving.

 Crabapples that are too small to use for baking work well here; the high ratio of skin gives the Crabapplejack a lovely, reddish-gold color.

8   See companion *Wild Berries & Fruits Field Guide of IN, KY and OH* – page 170

Apple or Crabapple Filling

Cinnamon and brown sugar give a wonderful flavor to this easy filling.

**1 cup cored, chopped apples or crabapples
(see note below for preparation tips)**

1½ tablespoons lemon juice

1½ tablespoons (packed) brown sugar

⅛ teaspoon cinnamon

In small, heavy-bottomed non-aluminum saucepan, combine apples or crabapples and lemon juice. Cover and cook over medium heat, stirring frequently, until fruit is tender, about 5 minutes. Stir in brown sugar and cinnamon; cook for about a minute longer to dissolve sugar. Cool before using.

Use this to prepare Easy Bear Claws (pg. 30), Fruit-Striped Cookie Fingers (pg. 145), or Fruit-Filled Muffins (pg. 163). Refrigerate extra filling, and use to top oatmeal or toast.

Note: To prepare the crabapples, cut each crab into quarters. Cut out the core, also removing the stems and blossom remnants; chop cleaned quarters by hand or in a mini food processor.

Aluminum and Non-Aluminum Cookware

Citrus juices, such as lemon or lime juice, are obviously high in acid, but even wild fruit juices have some acid. Aluminum reacts with acid to create undesirable flavors; the acid also dissolves minute particles of aluminum into the food, which may be a health concern. Many recipes in this book call for the use of non-aluminum cookware. Stainless steel and Pyrex® are good choices; this type of cookware is sometimes called "non-reactive" because it doesn't react with acids.

Apple Donut Holes

Donut "holes" are actually round donut balls, dropped from a spoon.

Vegetable oil for deep frying (about 1 quart)

2 cups all-purpose flour

1½ teaspoons baking powder

½ teaspoon salt

¼ teaspoon cinnamon

¼ teaspoon baking soda

⅓ cup applesauce

1 egg

1 tablespoon vegetable oil

⅔ cup (packed) brown sugar

3 tablespoons cream or half-and-half

½ cup finely chopped fresh apple

1 cup sugar mixed with 2 teaspoons cinnamon

Begin heating 2½ inches of oil in a deep fryer or heavy pot; it needs to be at 370°F when you start frying. Line a baking sheet with newspaper, then cover with paper towels; set aside. Place wire-mesh strainer over a large mixing bowl. Add flour, baking powder, salt, cinnamon and baking soda; shake to sift together into bowl. In a separate mixing bowl, combine applesauce, egg and 1 tablespoon oil; beat with hand mixer until smooth. Add brown sugar and cream; beat until smooth. Pour into flour mixture, then add chopped apple; stir with wooden spoon until well blended.

Using two tablespoons, pick up enough batter to form a ball about the size of a small walnut, rounding it between the tablespoons. Use one tablespoon to slide it off the other into the 370°F oil. Working quickly, shape and add two more balls. Use a long-handled slotted spoon to roll the balls over in the oil almost continuously; adjust heat to maintain oil temperature at 360°–365°F. Cook until donuts are nicely browned, about 3 minutes, then remove with slotted spoon, draining for a few seconds over the fryer before transferring to the prepared baking sheet. Cut into the first one to check doneness, and adjust size of dough ball if necessary so the donuts cook before they over-brown. Continue with remaining dough, cooking three at a time and maintaining the oil at 360°–365°F during frying. Roll donut holes in cinnamon-sugar.

Substitution: Substitute ½ cup persimmon purée for the applesauce; eliminate the chopped apple. Proceed as directed.

Crabapple-Ginger-Cardamom Jam

5 half-pints

Sparkling, bright red and tangy, this jam is a favorite of all who try it.

2 pounds crabapples

1 piece peeled fresh gingerroot, about 1 x 3 inches or slightly larger

3⅓ cups sugar

2 cups water

2 tablespoons freshly squeezed lemon juice

¾ teaspoon cardamom seeds (from about 15 cardamom pods)

Prepare 5 half-pint canning jars, bands and lids as directed on pg. 185. Cut crabapples into quarters; remove and discard cores. If crabapples are ½ inch in diameter or smaller, no further preparation is necessary; if crabapples are larger, cut each quarter in half from top to bottom so you have narrower wedges. Place crabapple wedges in heavy-bottomed non-aluminum pan. Grate gingerroot and add to pan along with remaining ingredients.

Heat to boiling over medium-high heat, stirring frequently. Reduce heat so mixture is bubbling at a moderate pace and cook, stirring frequently, until thickened, 45 minutes to 1 hour; a small scoop of jam should jell as described in Green Gooseberry Jam on pg. 66. Ladle into prepared jars, leaving ½ inch headspace. Seal with prepared lids and bands. Process in a water-bath canner (pg. 185) for 10 minutes.

Variation: Substitute 1¾ pounds apples, cut into ½-inch pieces, for the crabapples; the jam may not be as colorful as the crabapple version, but it tastes just as good.

Other recipes in this book featuring apples and crabapples:
Fruits of the Forest Pie, pg. 170
Six Recipes Using Wild Fruit Juice or Syrup, pgs. 172–176
Wild Berry or Fruit Syrup, pg. 177
Dehydrating Wild Berries and Fruits, pgs. 182–184
As a substitute in Autumn Olive "Berries" for Baking, pg. 14
As a substitute in Blackberry-Apple Crisp, pg. 21
As a substitute in Easy Cherry Applesauce, pg. 45
As a substitute in Hawthorn and Sausage Brunch Casserole, pg. 83
As a substitute in Pear Butter, pg. 123
As a substitute in Rose Hip-Apple Jelly, pg. 149
As a variation in Hawthorn Jelly, pg. 84

Quick ideas for using apples and crabapples:
Apple or crabapple juice mixes well with other wild fruit juices for making jelly.

AUTUMN OLIVE (Elaeagnus umbellata)

Here's a fruit that doesn't look—or cook—like anything you can buy in the store. Ripe fruits are soft and red, and covered with silvery scales; they look like they've been rolled in a subtle glitter. Fruits are borne profusely on the shrubs, so it's easy to gather a good quantity; a step ladder will help you reach fruits near the top. Choose fruits that are soft and red; unripe fruits aren't sweet. Fruit quality varies from plant to plant; sample a few before harvesting fruits from a particular plant to be sure they are sweet enough.

Some amateur winemakers use autumn olive fruit to make a light red wine. An Internet search for "autumn olive wine" will provide a number of recipes to try.

Autumn olive fruits have a large, hard pit; some foragers eat the whole fruit including the pit, although most make juice or purée. The pit can be removed by cooking the fruits, then straining or puréeing the mixture. For purée with a fresher taste, you can process the fruits through a food mill without cooking first; they're juicy enough that they don't need cooking to soften them first (although the yield will be slightly higher if the fruit is cooked because the added water helps separate the flesh from the pits). I've also heard that a juicer works well on autumn olives, to prepare fresh (uncooked) juice; I've never tried this, but if you have a juicer, give it a go.

When I'm making purée, I remove the stemlets before any processing, whether I'm cooking the fruits or not. Some don't bother, but I don't like small bits of stem in my finished purée, and feel it is worth the time. It works best to pinch the stem off with your fingernails rather than pull it off; the soft fruit may split from the pressure of pulling.

To make uncooked autumn olive purée, place fruits (preferably with the stems removed) in a food mill set over a large bowl; it's easiest to work with no more than 2 cups at a time. Turn the paddle until the fruits are smashed and as much pulp as possible has passed through the screen into the bowl. The large pits prevent all of the pulp from going through because the pulp is trapped around the pits and the paddle can't reach it. Now use a stiff rubber spatula to press the softened pulp through the holes; the spatula is much better for working around the hard pits. Processed in this fashion, a quart of ripe fruit will yield about 1 cup of thick, rich red purée that resembles tomato paste.

To prepare juice or cooked purée, measure the fruit and place in a non-aluminum pot; for juice, it's not necessary to remove the stemlets but for purée, it's preferable to remove them as described above. For juice, add 3 cups water per quart of fruit; for purée, add 1 cup water per quart of fruit. Heat to boiling, then reduce the heat; cover and simmer for about 10 minutes, gently crushing the fruit with a potato masher near the end of cooking. **For juice,** transfer the mixture to a strainer lined with doubled, dampened cheesecloth and let it drip for 30 minutes; if you're making jelly, don't squeeze the fruit or the jelly will be cloudy. After the clear liquid has dripped away, set it aside and squeeze the fruit into a different container; you can use this slightly cloudy juice as a beverage or for cooking. **For purée,** process the cooked fruit through a food mill, pressing with a rubber spatula as noted above. Processed this way, a quart of fruit will yield about 3½ cups of lovely red juice, or about 1½ cups of purée that is thinner than the purée from uncooked fruit.

Sweet Autumn Olive Bread

8 to 10 servings

This bread has a sweet surprise in the center: a layer of brown sugar and nuts. Prepared buttermilk baking mix makes it quick and easy to prepare.

⅓ cup (packed) brown sugar

½ cup chopped walnuts, hickory nuts or other nuts

¼ teaspoon nutmeg

3 eggs

3 tablespoons vegetable oil

3 tablespoons cream

¾ cup autumn olive purée from cooked fruits (see note below)

⅔ cup white sugar

2¼ cups buttermilk baking mix

Heat oven to 350°F. Spray a standard-sized loaf pan generously with nonstick spray; set aside. In small bowl, combine brown sugar, nuts and nutmeg, mixing well with your fingers or a fork; set aside.

Add eggs, oil and cream to a mixing bowl; beat well with fork. Add autumn olive purée and white sugar, and beat together. Add baking mix, and stir with the fork until mix is completely moistened; there may still be a few small lumps in the batter.

Pour half of the batter into the prepared loaf pan, spreading evenly. Sprinkle brown sugar mixture evenly over batter; top with remaining batter. Bake for 50 to 60 minutes, or until toothpick inserted in center comes out clean. Remove from oven and let stand 10 minutes. Run a table knife around the edges to loosen, then turn out onto plate. Let cool for at least 1 hour before slicing.

If you've made your autumn olive purée from uncooked fruits, it will be a bit thicker than it should be for this recipe. Use a bit less than ¾ cup of the thicker purée, and add a little water to thin it a bit.

Autumn Olive "Berries" for Baking
About ¼ cup "berries" per ½ cup purée

Autumn olives are generally not used whole for baking or recipes, as you could use, say, blueberries. The large, hard pits are usually removed first, and by the time that's done, what's left is just a small pile of wet skin with a little pulp. Here's a way to turn fruit purée into raisin-like morsels, which can be used in muffins or quick breads.

The "berries" are prepared from purée that is shaped, then dried in a dehydrator or your oven. Before starting, please read the section on dehydrating berries and fruits (pg. 182). Purée made from uncooked autumn olive fruits is thick enough to make the berries with no cooking. But if your purée was made with cooked fruits, or if you're substituting thinner purée from a different fruit, you'll have to cook the purée in a saucepan until it thickens before making the berries. It needs to be almost as thick as tomato paste, and there should be no liquid oozing around the bottom when you stir the purée.

Start with only one-third of the purée you want to use. Drop the purée in small rounded mounds, about the size of a canned kidney bean, onto a liner sheet if using a dehydrator, or onto a baking sheet lined with plastic wrap if using the oven. Keep ½ inch between the drops so they don't run together. Dry at 145°–150°F for 2 hours; keep remaining purée in the refrigerator during this time.

After 2 hours, use half of the remaining purée to spoon another kidney-bean-sized mound onto the drops that you've been drying. Dry for another 2 or 3 hours, or until the drops are solid enough to flip over (use a table knife if necessary to scrape the drops off the liner, then flip them). Spoon remaining purée on top of the flipped drops. Dry until firm and no longer sticky, typically another 3 to 5 hours; total drying time is 7 to 10 hours, but this varies depending on how wet the purée was. When berries are completely dry, transfer to a glass jar. Store in a cool place, checking several times in the first week to make sure they aren't emitting any moisture; if there is any moisture in the jar, return berries to dehydrator and dry some more. For storage longer than a few weeks, store in freezer.

Substitutions: You may substitute thick purée from highbush cranberries, crabapples, blackhaws, persimmons or other fruits (cooked to thicken if necessary, as described above) for the autumn olive purée.

 These "berries" don't hold up in pie, sauce or other long-simmered dishes; they turn back into purée.

Refrigerator Cookies with Autumn Olive "Berries"

About 24 cookies

The nutmeg and brandy add a delightfully different taste to these crisp, buttery cookies. Make a batch of the dough in the morning and pop it in the refrigerator. Later in the day, it'll be easy to slice off and have fresh-baked cookies for an after-school snack.

½ cup (1 stick) unsalted butter, softened

¾ cup sugar

1 egg

1 tablespoon brandy or cognac, or ¼ teaspoon brandy flavoring

½ teaspoon nutmeg

1¾ cups all-purpose flour

⅓ to ½ cup dried autumn olive "berries"

In mixing bowl, cream butter with electric mixer until light and fluffy. Add sugar; beat until fluffy. Add egg and beat well. Add brandy and nutmeg; beat until smooth. In another mixing bowl, combine flour and dried berries; stir to blend. Add flour mixture to butter mixture; stir with a wooden spoon until soft dough forms (do not over-mix, or the cookies will be tough). Transfer dough to a 1-gallon zipper-style food storage bag. Using your hands to press the dough together from the outside, form it into a firmly packed cylinder at the bottom of the bag, rolling it on the counter to smooth the shape; it will be about 2 inches around. Seal the bag and refrigerate for at least 5 hours, or overnight.

When you're ready to bake, heat oven to 350°F. Line 2 baking sheets with kitchen parchment, or spray with nonstick spray. Slit the plastic bag open to expose the roll of dough. Use a very sharp knife to cut the roll into ¼-inch-thick slices; transfer to prepared baking sheets. Bake for 10 minutes, then rotate pans (see "Rotating Cookies while Baking," below). Continue baking until lightly browned around the edges, 9 to 13 minutes longer. Transfer to wire rack to cool.

Variation: Refrigerator Cookies with Dried Berries
Follow recipe above, substituting dried blueberries, raspberries, serviceberries, muscadines or strawberries for the autumn olive "berries."

Rotating Cookies while Baking

If you're baking more than one sheet of cookies, they tend to bake unevenly because the pan on top blocks heat to the pan (or pans) below it. To help ensure even cooking, rotate the pans about halfway through baking, moving the top pan to the lower shelf and moving the lower pan to the top shelf; as you do this, also rotate the pans so the edge that was at the front of the oven is now in the back of the oven.

Autumn Olive Jelly

4 half-pints

3 cups autumn olive juice

1 tablespoon lemon juice

Half of a 1.75-ounce box powdered pectin

½ teaspoon butter, optional (helps reduce foaming)

3¼ cups sugar

Prepare and process as directed in Jelly Instructions (using pectin), pg. 178.

Autumn Olive Jam

3 half-pints

2 cups autumn olive purée

Half of a 1.75-ounce box powdered pectin

2 tablespoons lemon juice

2¾ cups sugar

Prepare and process as directed in Jam Instructions (using pectin), pg. 181.

Other recipes in this book featuring autumn olives:
Six Recipes Using Wild Fruit Juice or Syrup, pgs. 172–176
Wild Berry or Fruit Syrup, pg. 177
Wild Berry or Fruit Leather, pg. 184

Quick ideas for using autumn olives:
Replace some of the cut-up apple with whole autumn olive fruits when making an apple pie; eat a few of the autumn olives first, to make sure that the pits aren't too hard, and alert diners of their presence.

BLACKBERRIES and DEWBERRIES

(Blackberries, *Rubus allegheniensis* and others; dewberries, *R. flagellaris, R. hispidus, R. pubescens* and others)

The common blackberry (*Rubus allegheniensis*) and the other blackberry varieties found in our area are the wild versions of the familiar fruit found in the supermarket; like many wild fruits, they are smaller than their domestic counterparts. Common (*R. flagellaris*) and bristly (*R. hispidus*) dewberries are two of the numerous species of dewberries that are black when ripe; red dewberries (*R. pubescens*) are red when ripe. All can be used in the same way. (To avoid cumbersome ingredients lists, the recipes on the following pages all call for blackberries, but you can use dewberries instead—or even a mix of two fruits.)

Blackberries and dewberries ripen in midsummer or later, when many other berries are finished. They seem to pick up extra taste over their slow ripening; although a bit less sweet than many other berries, they have a deeper, more interesting flavor.

One thing that these fruits have in common are seeds . . . lots and lots of them. They're harder than seeds found in raspberries, and can make jam or desserts seem almost crunchy. Some people prefer to strain cooked or crushed blackberries to remove the seeds. For most dishes, I like the texture that the whole or lightly crushed fruits provide. (See pg. 23 for a jam recipe that is a compromise; half of the seeds are strained out, while the rest of the fruit provides texture to the jam.)

To prepare purée or juice, measure the fruit and place in a non-aluminum pot. For purée, add ½ cup water per quart of fruit; for juice, add 1 cup water per quart of fruit. Gently crush the fruit with a potato masher to start the juices flowing. Heat to boiling, then reduce the heat; cover and simmer for about 10 minutes. **For seedless purée,** process the cooked fruit through a food mill, then discard the seeds; if you don't mind the seeds, the purée is ready after cooking. **For juice,** transfer the mixture to a strainer lined with doubled, dampened cheesecloth and let it drip for 30 minutes; if you're making jelly, don't squeeze the fruit or the jelly will be cloudy. After the clear liquid has dripped away, set it aside and squeeze the fruit into a different container; you can use this slightly cloudy juice as a beverage or for cooking. Processed this way, a quart of fruit will yield about 1½ cups of purée, or about 2 cups of juice.

Blackberries and dewberries can be frozen for later use in jam, pies and other cooked desserts. Simply lay them on a baking sheet in a single layer and freeze; when the berries are solid, pack them into plastic bags or freezer containers for storage.

Blackberry Turnovers

4 turnovers

Wild blackberries are much smaller than domestic blackberries, and tuck nicely into these individual turnovers.

1½ cups fresh blackberries (about 7 ounces)

⅓ cup shredded Granny Smith apple (about one-quarter of an apple)

3 tablespoons sugar, plus additional for sprinkling on crust

1 tablespoon all-purpose flour, plus additional for rolling out pastry

Ready-to-use pastry for single-crust pie

A little cream for brushing turnovers

Heat oven to 375°F. In mixing bowl, combine blackberries, shredded apple, 3 tablespoons sugar and 1 tablespoon flour. Stir gently to mix; set aside for 10 minutes.

While fruit is standing, prepare crusts: Divide pastry into 4 equal portions and shape each into a ball. On a lightly floured worksurface, roll each into a circle about 6 inches across. Divide fruit mixture evenly between circles, mounding in center. Brush edges lightly with water. Fold each circle in half; seal edges well with a fork. Place on baking sheet. Brush tops lightly with cream; sprinkle with sugar. Make several small slits in the top of each turnover. Bake until crust is golden brown and the filling is bubbling in the slits, 25 to 30 minutes.

Smooth Blackberry Sauce

About 1 cup

This type of sauce is sometimes called a coulis. *It's excellent when used to top ice cream, French toast or cooked cereal. For an elegant dessert, spoon a puddle of the sauce onto individual dessert plates, then top with a piece of cheesecake or a poached pear.*

1 cup strained, seedless blackberry purée

¼ to ½ cup sugar

**⅛ teaspoon grated lemon zest
(colored rind only, with none of the white pith)**

In small, heavy-bottomed non-aluminum saucepan, combine purée, ¼ cup sugar, and the lemon zest. Heat over medium-high heat, stirring constantly, until boiling. Cook, stirring constantly, until purée has thickened to a sauce-like consistency. Taste, and add additional sugar if needed; if you do add more sugar, cook the sauce for another few minutes, stirring constantly, to dissolve the sugar. Cool before using.

Wild Berry Vinegar

Use in salad dressings, or in marinades for poultry, meat or fish. This makes a lovely gift.

1 pint blackberries, raspberries, strawberries, elderberries or highbush cranberries

1 quart white wine vinegar

You'll need a glass bottle that holds at least 2 quarts for this, with a mouth wide enough to insert the berries; juice is often sold in these types of bottles. Wash it very well, then fill it with boiling water and let stand for at least 5 minutes.

Drain water from bottle; add berries. In medium saucepan, heat vinegar over low heat until it just begins to steam; don't let vinegar boil. Pour warm vinegar over berries in bottle. Let stand until cooled to room temperature, then seal bottle and shake gently. Set bottle in dark, cool place for 1 week, shaking occasionally. Strain through a sieve lined with a coffee filter into clean 1-quart measuring cup with a spout; discard berries. Pour vinegar into a clean bottle. It will keep, at room temperature, for at least 6 months.

 For a more decorative presentation, spear a few fresh berries and a curl of lemon zest on a wooden skewer; place skewer in the storage bottle before adding strained, finished vinegar to the bottle. (Be sure to wash the lemon well before making the zest curl.)

Blackberry Sidecar

This is a strong drink, so try it when you don't have anywhere to drive!

2 ounces gin

1 ounce triple sec liqueur

1 tablespoon blackberry syrup (pg. 177)

1 tablespoon lime juice

2 or 3 fresh blackberries for garnish, optional

Combine gin, triple sec, blackberry syrup and lime juice in a shaker filled with crushed ice. Cover and shake well. Strain into a chilled cocktail glass; garnish with fresh blackberries. Call a cab.

Blackberry Filling

This filling is dark, thick, glossy and totally luscious.

½ teaspoon water

½ teaspoon cornstarch

6 ounces fresh or previously frozen blackberries (about 1¼ cups)

1 tablespoon grated apple

1½ tablespoons sugar

In small bowl, blend together water and cornstarch; set aside. In small, heavy-bottomed non-aluminum saucepan, combine blackberries, apple and sugar. Crush fruit gently with a potato masher to start juices flowing. Heat to boiling over medium-high heat, then cook, stirring frequently, until mixture is no longer runny; this will take 9 to 11 minutes. Add cornstarch mixture, stirring constantly; cook for about 1 minute longer, or until thick. Cool completely before using.

Use this to prepare Easy Bear Claws (pg. 30), Fruit-Striped Cookie Fingers (pg. 145), or Fruit-Filled Muffins (pg. 163). Refrigerate extra filling, and use to top oatmeal or toast.

Blackberry Jelly

4 half-pints

2¾ cups blackberry juice

2 tablespoons lemon juice

Two-thirds of a 1.75-ounce box powdered pectin

½ teaspoon butter, optional (helps reduce foaming)

3½ cups sugar

Prepare and process as directed in Jelly Instructions (using pectin), pg. 178.

Blackberry-Apple Crisp

9 servings

The combination of blackberries and apples makes a wonderful crisp—the color is lovely, and the mix of tart and sweet is just right. Serve with a scoop of vanilla ice cream.

2 large cooking apples such as Granny Smith, Fireside or McIntosh

2 cups fresh or previously frozen blackberries (about 10 ounces)

2 teaspoons cornstarch

½ cup all-purpose flour

½ cup (packed) golden brown sugar

½ teaspoon cinnamon

¼ teaspoon nutmeg

4 tablespoons (half of a stick) cold butter, cut into pieces

¼ cup quick-cooking rolled oats

Heat oven to 375°F. Spray 8-inch-square baking dish with nonstick spray. Peel and core apples, then chop them coarsely in food processor or by hand; place in prepared dish. Add blackberries and cornstarch; stir gently to mix. Set aside.

In mixing bowl, combine flour, brown sugar, cinnamon and nutmeg; stir to mix. Add butter; blend with your fingertips (or a fork) until the mixture is the texture of very coarse sand, with a few pea-sized pieces of butter remaining. Stir in rolled oats. Sprinkle the mixture evenly over the fruit. Bake until topping is golden-brown and filling bubbles, 35 to 45 minutes. Let cool on wire rack at least 15 minutes before serving; serve warm or at room temperature.

Substitutions: Blueberries, serviceberries or raspberries may be substituted for the blackberries in this simple crisp. Wild apples can be substituted for the cooking apples; you'll need about 2 cups of chopped apple.

When making the topping for a crisp, don't over-mix or make it too fine. It's easiest to sprinkle when it's still got some coarse bits in it, and it comes out with a better texture than if it is well blended.

Blackberry Freezer Jam

4 half-pints

The fruit is not cooked when preparing this easy jam; it has a fresh, vibrant flavor.

1 quart blackberries

1¾ cups sugar

**Two-thirds of a 1.75-ounce box powdered pectin
(see pg. 178 for information on dividing pectin)**

⅔ cup water

Prepare 4 half-pint canning jars, bands and lids as described on pg. 185, or have clean plastic freezer containers ready (see tip below). Crush fruit with a potato masher in a mixing bowl, or chop to medium consistency in food processor (don't overprocess; jam should have small fruit chunks in it). Measure 1¾ cups crushed or chopped fruit; use any leftover fruit to top ice cream or cook in other recipes. Place measured fruit and the sugar in a large ceramic or Pyrex® mixing bowl. Stir well; set aside for 10 minutes, stirring several times with a wooden spoon.

When fruit has rested for 10 minutes, prepare pectin. In small non-aluminum saucepan, combine pectin and water; stir well (mixture may be lumpy). Heat to a full, rolling boil over high heat, stirring constantly. Cook at a rolling boil for 1 minute, stirring constantly. Pour pectin mixture into fruit in bowl. Stir constantly with a wooden spoon until sugar is completely dissolved and no longer grainy, about 3 minutes; a few grains may remain, but the mixture should no longer look cloudy (or the jam will be cloudy).

Pour into prepared jars or containers, leaving ½ inch headspace; cover with clean lids. Let stand at room temperature for 24 hours; the jam should set (it may be softer than regular jam, especially at first; that's okay). If jam is not set, refrigerate for several days until set before using or freezing. Use within 3 weeks, or freeze until needed; thaw frozen jam in refrigerator.

Special plastic containers, designed especially for freezing jam and jelly, are available with the canning supplies at the supermarket.

Smoother Blackberry Jam

4 half-pints

Blackberry jam has a wonderful, deep flavor, but some find it too seedy to enjoy. This recipe removes about half of the seeds; this leaves enough whole berries for a good texture.

5 cups fresh blackberries

2 tablespoons lemon juice

Half of a 1.75-ounce package powdered pectin

3¼ cups sugar

Place blackberries in mixing bowl; crush with potato masher. Transfer half of the crushed berries to a wire-mesh strainer set over another mixing bowl; press through with wooden spoon to strain seeds. Measure strained blackberries; add crushed blackberries to equal 2½ cups. Transfer measured fruit to 3-quart (or larger) heavy-bottomed non-aluminum pot (reserve any remaining fruit to top ice cream). Prepare and process as directed in Jam Instructions (using pectin), pg. 181.

Other recipes in this book featuring blackberries or dewberries:
Rice Pudding with Wild Berries, pg. 103
Fruits of the Forest Pie, pg. 170
Brambleberry Cream Sauce, pg. 171
Six Recipes Using Wild Fruit Juice or Syrup, pgs. 172–176
Wild Berry or Fruit Syrup, pg. 177
Wild Berry or Fruit Leather, pg. 184
As a variation in Mulberry Ripple Cheesecake, pg. 100
As a variation in Persimmon Smoothie, pg. 131

Quick ideas for using blackberries or dewberries:
When making apple pie, reduce the amount of apples by 1 cup and add a cup of fresh or previously frozen blackberries or dewberries.

BLACKHAWS, NANNYBERRIES and WITHE-ROD
(Viburnum prunifolium , V. lentago and V. cassinoides)

Blackhaws and nannyberries are very similar in appearance and eating quality. A third related plant, withe-rod (V. cassinoides), is found occasionally in our area; it is sometimes called "wild raisin" because in its dried, wrinkled state, it resembles the common domestic fruit. All three can be handled in the same way in the kitchen. They make excellent trail nibbles when fully ripe and soft; even when the fruits dry and shrivel later in the season, they are still tasty, with a flavor that is somewhat like a prune with tropical overtones.

It's best to pick these fruits when they are ripe and plump, before they dry and shrivel. They're still edible in the dried state, and make a delicious snack; but if you're making purée, your yield will be poor if you work with dried fruits.

Withe-rod is blue-black when ripe, while nannyberry and blackhaw are a deeper black. Fruits of all three grow in flat-topped clusters; when you find a plant with ripe fruit, it's easy to harvest a good quantity by snipping off the entire cluster. If there are a few underripe fruits on the cluster, leave the cluster out at room temperature for a few days, where the fruits will ripen completely; the ripe fruits on the cluster will be fine while the others ripen, so you don't need to separate them. Store ripe fruits in the refrigerator, where they'll keep for several weeks.

All three fruits are excellent raw, eaten out-of-hand as a snack, although the large, flat seed is inedible and must be spit out (think of it like watermelon; the seeds are similar). The fruits also make an outstanding purée or nectar. Pick the fruits off the stems, then measure them and place in a heavy-bottomed, non-aluminum pot. Add 3 cups water per quart of picked fruit. **For puree,** heat to boiling, then reduce heat and simmer gently, uncovered, for about 45 minutes. Process through a food mill while still warm, then discard the seeds. A quart of ripe, but not dry, fruit produces 2 to 3 cups of thick, luscious purée; yield will be considerably less if the fruit is dry when processed.

For nectar, reduce simmering time to 20 minutes; cover the pan during simmering. Process through the food mill (or a conical strainer). Scrape the pulpy seed mixture remaining in the food mill back into the cooking pot, and add about ¾ cup water; stir well to loosen the pulp. Return mixture to the food mill and process again, combining the two batches of resulting purée. You should get 3 to 4 cups of nectar.

Purées of blackhaw, nannyberry and withe-rod make an excellent, jam-like spread with no further processing (other than some additional sweetening if you like); they're rather like apple butter. They can also be used for baking, sauces and other delicious dishes. To avoid cumbersome ingredients lists, the recipes on the following pages all call for blackhaw purée or nectar, but purée and nectar made from nannyberries or withe-rod may be substituted in equal amounts, with great results.

Blackhaw Carrot Cake

Blackhaw nectar gives a rich, deep color and delightful sweetness to this cake. It's great just as it is, but if you like, you can top it with Cream Cheese Frosting (pg. 87) or serve it with lightly sweetened whipped cream.

2 cups all-purpose flour

1 teaspoon baking soda

¾ teaspoon cinnamon

½ teaspoon salt

3 eggs

1⅓ cups sugar

½ cup vegetable oil

¾ cup blackhaw nectar

1 teaspoon vanilla extract

2¼ cups grated raw carrots

1 cup chopped walnuts, hickory nuts or pecans

Heat oven to 350°F. Grease and flour 9x13-inch baking dish; set aside. Sift together flour, baking soda, cinnamon and salt. In mixing bowl, combine eggs, sugar, oil, blackhaw nectar and vanilla. Beat with electric mixer until smooth. Add flour mixture; stir with a wooden spoon just until combined. Add carrots and nuts; stir just until combined. Scrape into prepared dish. Bake until a toothpick inserted in the center comes out clean, 40 to 50 minutes. Serve warm or at room temperature.

Egg Talk
Recipes in this book simply call for "eggs" without distinguishing between sizes. For best results, use large eggs, rather than medium or small eggs. If you are watching cholesterol, you may substitute ¼ cup liquid egg substitute for each egg in a recipe; it works great in place of whole eggs in all dishes except custards.

Blackhaw Barbecue Sauce

1 cup

This easy sauce gets a rich, sweet taste from the blackhaws.

- **¾ cup blackhaw purée**
- **2 tablespoons honey**
- **1½ tablespoons Dijon mustard**
- **2 teaspoons lemon juice**
- **1½ teaspoons crumbled, dried thyme**
- **½ teaspoon salt, or to taste**
- **¼ teaspoon freshly ground black pepper, or to taste**

In small mixing bowl, combine all ingredients; stir well and refrigerate until needed. This will keep for a month in the refrigerator.

 Use this with pork or chicken, as you would regular barbecue sauce. See below for a simple grilled pork chop recipe as an example.

Pork Loin Chops with Blackhaw Barbecue Sauce

4 servings

Putting the sauce on the chops after they're turned prevents it from burning.

- **4 boneless pork loin chops (about 6 ounces each)**
- **Salt and pepper**
- **2 to 3 tablespoons Blackhaw Barbecue Sauce**

Prepare grill for direct, medium heat (see "Grilling: Direct vs. Indirect Heat," pg. 27). Season chops lightly on both sides with salt and pepper. Place on grate directly over heat; cover and cook for about 3 minutes, until nicely marked. Rotate chops 90 degrees, keeping the same side down; re-cover and cook for about 2 minutes longer. Turn chops. Spoon a generous amount of sauce over each chop. Re-cover grill and cook until chops are cooked through, 3 to 8 minutes depending on thickness of chops.

Grilling: Direct vs. Indirect Heat

When preparing your charcoal or gas grill, you can set it up for direct or indirect heat. Direct heat works well for foods that need hot, quick cooking; indirect heat is better for those that need longer cooking and would burn if exposed directly to the hottest part of the fire.

For direct cooking with charcoal, pile a good quantity of coals in the center of the grill and light them; when they are covered with ash, spread them out just a bit, and put the food directly over the coals. For direct cooking with gas, light one or more burners and preheat on high; when the grill is hot, place the food directly over the hot burner still set on high.

For indirect cooking with charcoal, pile coals to one side of the grill and light them; when they are covered with ash, spread them out evenly over half of the grill, and put the food over the half of the grill that has no coals. For indirect cooking with gas, light one burner and preheat on high; when the grill is hot, reduce heat slightly and place the food on the grate away from the lit area. Some recipes call for browning meat over direct heat, then moving it to the cooler, indirect side to finish cooking.

Blackhaw Filling

About ½ cup; easily increased

⅓ cup blackhaw purée

2 tablespoons golden raisins

2 tablespoons (packed) brown sugar

**½ teaspoon grated orange zest
(colored rind only, not the white pith), optional**

Combine all ingredients in small bowl; mix well.

Use this to prepare Easy Bear Claws (pg. 30), Fruit-Striped Cookie Fingers (pg. 145), or Fruit-Filled Muffins (pg. 163). Refrigerate extra filling, and use to top oatmeal or toast.

Other recipes in this book featuring blackhaws, nannyberries and withe-rod:
Wild Berry or Fruit Leather, pg. 184
As a substitute in Autumn Olive "Berries" for Baking, pg. 14

Quick ideas for using blackhaws, nannyberries and withe-rod:
Sweeten a batch of nectar, prepared as directed on pg. 24, to taste; chill and serve as a delicious breakfast drink.
Add a handful of whole fruits to cut-up apples when making applesauce; note that this works only with recipes that call for cooking and then straining the apples to remove the seeds.
Sweeten the purée a bit, and serve on top of hot oatmeal.

BLUEBERRIES and HUCKLEBERRIES
(Blueberries, *Vaccinium* spp.; huckleberries, *Gaylussacia baccata*)

Blueberries are probably the wild fruit that is picked most often in our area. They are widespread in our region, and the wild fruits look just like a small version of the familiar domestic fruits; they're delicious raw or cooked. Huckleberries are much less familiar, but equally delicious, and can be used in the same way as blueberries. Deerberries (*V. stamineum*) and farkleberries (*V. arboreum*) are related to blueberries, and have similar fruits. Deerberries can be used like blueberries, although fruits from individual plants may be bitter, suited to jam-making or best left for woodland creatures. Farkleberries tend to be tough and mealy and are generally not eaten, although a few added to a baked dish won't spoil it.

You need to look both low and high when searching for these tasty fruits. Most blueberries in our area are short shrubs, but highbush blueberries are present in some areas. Huckleberries are small shrubs, generally 3 feet or less.

Wild blueberries have more flavor than domestic blueberries, probably because they are smaller and have more of the flavorful skin in proportion to the flesh. If you're substituting wild blueberries in a recipe that was written for domestic blueberries, use a bit less by volume than called for; the smaller wild blueberries pack more closely in the measuring cup, so a cup of wild blueberries weighs more than a cup of domestic blueberries. The other fruits listed here are similar in size to wild blueberries, and a bit less juicy. (To avoid cumbersome ingredients lists, the recipes that follow all call for blueberries; feel free to use any of the listed fruits.)

It's easy to gather a decent quantity of wild blueberries, once you've found a good patch; the others listed here tend to be more scattered, so you might end up mixing them with your wild blueberry haul to get a sufficient quantity for use in recipes. Blueberries and huckleberries are among the first plants to grow in an area that has been swept by wildfire; if you can travel to an area that burned the previous year, you should enjoy phenomenal blueberry and huckleberry picking.

Blueberries and huckleberries have soft seeds that are virtually unnoticeable, and can be eaten raw or cooked. They're rich in anthocyanins, antioxidants believed to reduce the risk of cancer and diabetes, promote heart health, and help prevent age-related memory loss. They store well in the refrigerator, remaining fresh for up to a week; don't wash them until you're ready to use them, though, or they may mold.

They're easy to freeze; simply wash and pat dry, then spread in a single layer on a baking sheet and freeze overnight. The next day, transfer the individually frozen berries to freezer containers, and freeze for up to 6 months. Finally, they can be successfully dried in a dehydrator, and used in trail mixes and as an out-of-hand snack, or to substitute for raisins or craisins in recipes. Most people prefer to use these berries whole, but they can be juiced; the juice is an excellent beverage, sweetened as needed, and can also be used to make jelly. To prepare juice, follow the instructions for making blackberry juice on pg. 17; to make jelly, follow the proportions for Autumn Olive Jelly on pg. 16.

Classic Blueberry Pie

1 pie (6 to 8 servings)

Wild blueberries give this traditional pie an exceptional flavor.

1 quart fresh or previously frozen blueberries

1 cup sugar

¼ cup quick-cooking tapioca

1 tablespoon lemon juice

½ teaspoon cinnamon

½ teaspoon nutmeg

Pinch of salt

Ready-to-use pastry for double-crust pie

2 tablespoons butter, cut into pieces

1 egg, lightly beaten

Heat oven to 375°F. In mixing bowl, combine blueberries, sugar, tapioca, lemon juice, cinnamon, nutmeg and salt. Stir gently until well mixed; set aside for 15 minutes.

Fit one pastry into ungreased deep-dish pie plate. Scrape blueberry mixture into pie plate. Scatter butter pieces over blueberries. Moisten edges of pastry in pie plate with a little cold water, then top with second pastry. Seal, trim and flute edges. Cut 6 to 8 inch-long slits in the crust. Place pie on baking sheet (to catch drips). Brush top with beaten egg. Bake until crust is golden and filling bubbles through slits, 35 to 40 minutes. Transfer to rack to cool; best served warm.

 For extra sparkle and flavor, sprinkle a tablespoon of sugar over the top crust after brushing it with the egg.

Easy Bear Claws

This quick version of a bakery staple uses refrigerated biscuits to eliminate complicated pastry-making. Quick, easy—and delicious.

1 tube (8 biscuits; 16.3 ounces) refrigerated "grand-sized" flaky biscuits (reduced-fat works fine)

All-purpose flour for rolling dough

½ cup Blueberry Filling (pg. 33), or other wild fruit filling (see "Filling options" below)

1 egg, beaten with 1 teaspoon water

¼ cup sliced almonds

2 tablespoons coarse sugar, such as turbinado

Heat oven to 375°F. Line 2 rimmed baking sheets with kitchen parchment; set aside.

Separate dough into 8 biscuits. On lightly floured worksurface, gently roll one into an oval that is 4 inches across and about 6 inches long. Spoon one-eighth of the filling mixture onto the center of the dough. Fold the dough over to make a half-moon. Press edges together very well, lifting the edge and pinching all around with your fingertips. Place on a prepared baking sheet. Repeat with remaining dough and filling, keeping at least 1 inch between the rolls.

With a very sharp knife, make 4 cuts through the sealed edge, cutting about halfway into the crescent. Fan the cut strips out slightly to resemble a bear's paw. Brush dough with beaten egg; sprinkle with almonds and sugar. Bake for 8 minutes, then switch the baking sheets so the one underneath moves to the top shelf. Continue baking until golden brown and cooked through, 9 to 12 minutes longer; when the rolls are properly cooked, the dough should not feel mushy when pressed gently with a fingertip. Remove from oven and let stand about a minute, then transfer rolls to wire rack to cool for at least 15 minutes before serving. Best served warm, the day they are made.

Filling options: This recipe works with any of the following fillings: Apple or Crabapple (pg. 9), Blackberry (pg. 20), Blackhaw (pg. 27), Blueberry (pg. 33), Green Gooseberry (pg. 67), Ground Cherry (pg. 76), Mulberry (pg. 101), Muscadine (pg. 107), Peach (pg. 119), Pear (pg.123), Persimmon (pg. 129), Plum (pg. 137), Raspberry (pg. 143), Serviceberry (pg. 156), or Strawberry (pg. 161). You may also use plain, unsweetened mashed pawpaws as a filling.

Be sure to buy the extra-large biscuits; standard-sized biscuits won't work here.

Blueberry Streusel Muffins

12 muffins

A tasty streusel topping adds interest to these delicious muffins.

Streusel

⅓ cup sugar

¼ cup all-purpose flour

½ teaspoon cinnamon

4 tablespoons (half of a stick) cold butter, cut into pieces

½ cup sugar

½ cup (1 stick) butter, softened

1 egg

1 teaspoon vanilla extract

2¼ cups all-purpose flour

1 tablespoon plus 1 teaspoon baking powder

¼ teaspoon salt

1 cup whole milk, divided

1 to 1¼ cups fresh or still-frozen blueberries (4½ to 5½ ounces)

Heat oven to 375°F. Line 12-cup muffin tin with paper liners; set aside. Make the streusel: In a small bowl, stir together the sugar, flour and cinnamon. Add butter; use a fork or your fingertips to blend the butter into the sugar mixture, working them together until mixture is the texture of very coarse sand with some pea-sized particles. Set aside.

In mixing bowl, beat sugar and butter with an electric mixer until fluffy. Add egg and vanilla; beat well. Place a wire-mesh strainer over a plate; add flour, baking powder and salt. Shake the strainer over the mixing bowl until half of the flour has been added to the butter mixture. Stir with a wooden spoon until just moistened. Add half of the milk; stir until combined. Add remaining flour and milk in the same manner. Add blueberries and stir very gently until incorporated. Spoon batter into prepared muffin cups. Spoon streusel over batter. Bake until golden brown and springy to the touch, 25 to 30 minutes.

Substitution: Use 1¼ cups serviceberries in place of the blueberries.

 If you're using frozen blueberries, don't thaw them before mixing into the batter; add them while still frozen. This prevents soggy, purple muffins.

Blueberry Jalousie (Window-Blind Tart)   6 servings

Frozen puff pastry makes this fancy-looking dessert easy to make; the instructions look complicated, but it's a snap to prepare.

1½ cups fresh or previously frozen blueberries (about 7 ounces)

1 medium apple, peeled, cored and chopped

2 tablespoons butter, cut into several pieces

1 tablespoon lemon juice

½ cup sugar

1 sheet frozen puff pastry (half of 17.3-ounce package), thawed according to package directions

A little all-purpose flour for rolling out dough

1 egg, beaten with a fork

2 teaspoons coarse sugar, such as turbinado, optional

In heavy-bottomed non-aluminum saucepan, combine blueberries, apple, butter and lemon juice. Heat over medium heat until fruits start to produce juices. Stir in sugar and cook, stirring frequently, until sugar dissolves and mixture is bubbling, about 3 minutes. Adjust heat so mixture is gently boiling and cook, stirring occasionally, until mixture is thick and no longer runny, about 15 minutes. Remove from heat and set aside until no longer hot, then refrigerate for at least an hour, or until cold (filling can be prepared a day in advance; transfer mixture to a bowl, then cover tightly and refrigerate until needed).

When you're ready to bake, heat oven to 400°F. Line a rimmed baking sheet with kitchen parchment. On lightly floured worksurface, roll puff pastry to a 12x12-inch rectangle; cut in half to make two 6x12-inch rectangles. Place 1 rectangle on prepared baking sheet; set aside. Sprinkle top of remaining rectangle with a little flour, then fold in half the long way (3x12 inches). Cut a slit about 1½ inches long in the middle of the sheet, cutting from the folded edge towards the outer edge. Cut 2 more slits on each side of the center slit (for a total of 5 slits), spacing the slits about 1¾ inches from the center slit and from each other; see diagram below.

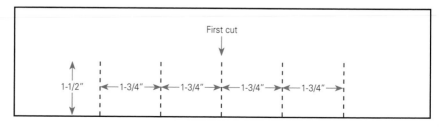

First cut

1-1/2"   ←—1-3/4"—→ ←—1-3/4"—→ ←—1-3/4"—→ ←—1-3/4"—→

Spoon cold blueberry mixture onto pastry that is on the baking sheet, leaving a 1-inch border. Brush border lightly with beaten egg. Place second pastry on top, aligning the uncut edge with one of the long edges of the bottom pastry. Unfold the pastry, aligning the edges; the slits should open slightly, revealing the filling. Press all edges together very well with a fork. Brush entire top of pastry with beaten egg, then sprinkle with the coarse sugar. Bake until golden brown, 25 to 30 minutes. Cool on baking sheet until lukewarm before using two large spatulas to transfer pastry to serving plate. Cut along the slits to serve.

 Plan your schedule so you can prepare the filling at least an hour before you plan to bake the tart; it needs to be cold when the tart is assembled. Apples help thicken the blueberry filling.

Blueberry Filling
About ½ cup; easily increased

½ teaspoon water

½ teaspoon cornstarch

6 ounces fresh or previously frozen blueberries (about 1⅓ cups)

1 heaping tablespoon grated apple

1 tablespoon sugar

In small bowl, blend together water and cornstarch; set aside. In small, heavy-bottomed saucepan, combine blueberries, apple and sugar. Crush fruit gently with a potato masher to start juices flowing. Heat to boiling over medium-high heat, then cook, stirring frequently and mashing once more, until mixture is no longer runny; this will take 8 to 10 minutes. Add cornstarch mixture, stirring constantly; cook for about 1 minute longer, or until thick. Cool before using.

Use this to prepare Easy Bear Claws (pg. 30), Fruit-Striped Cookie Fingers (pg. 145), or Fruit-Filled Muffins (pg. 163). Refrigerate extra filling, and use to top oatmeal or toast.

Wild Blueberry Pancakes

When wild blueberries are on the breakfast menu, it's worth taking the few extra minutes to whip up a homemade batter.

1 cup whole milk

1½ teaspoons freshly squeezed lemon juice

1 cup plus 2 tablespoons all-purpose flour

1 tablespoon powdered sugar

1¼ teaspoons baking powder

¼ teaspoon salt

2 tablespoons unsalted butter, melted and cooled slightly

1 egg

Nonstick cooking spray (or vegetable oil)

⅔ cup fresh blueberries (about 3 ounces)

Butter and syrup for serving

In 2-cup measure, stir together milk and lemon juice; set aside while you prepare the other ingredients. Begin heating a griddle over medium heat.

Place a wire-mesh strainer over a mixing bowl. Add flour, powdered sugar, baking powder and salt to strainer; shake to sift into bowl. Add butter and egg to milk; beat with a fork until well blended. Pour all at once into flour mixture; stir with the fork until batter is just combined. Don't over-mix; there should be a number of small lumps in the batter.

Spray hot griddle with nonstick spray (or brush with vegetable oil). Pour batter in ¼-cup batches onto griddle. Immediately scatter about 1 tablespoon of blueberries over each pancake. Cook until bottom is nicely browned and spotted, and top side has numerous small bubbles beginning to appear. Flip carefully and cook second side until spotted with brown. Transfer to a warm serving plate; cover loosely and keep warm while you cook remaining pancakes. Serve hot, with butter and syrup.

Variation: To use frozen berries, substitute ⅔ cup frozen blueberries for the fresh berries. While berries are still frozen, place them into a wire-mesh strainer and rinse them briefly under cool water, then spread out in a single layer on a paper towel to dry while you prepare the batter.

 Adding the berries to the pancake once it's on the griddle prevents soggy, purple pancakes. This recipe also works beautifully with wild strawberries.

Blueberry Spirals with Cardamom

8 rolls

Cardamom adds an unusual touch to these rolls. Plan on eating these with a knife and fork, to get every bit of the delicious berry filling.

1 loaf (1 pound) frozen bread dough, thawed according to package directions

All-purpose flour for rolling out dough

2 tablespoons butter, softened

1 cup fresh blueberries (about 4½ ounces)

½ cup chopped pecans

3 tablespoons sugar

½ teaspoon ground cardamom

¼ teaspoon cinnamon

Spray an 8x12-inch baking dish with nonstick spray; set aside. Roll bread dough on lightly floured worksurface into a rectangle about 8 inches by 12 inches. Spread butter evenly over bread. Sprinkle blueberries and pecans over bread, keeping an inch away from the long edges. In a small bowl, stir together the sugar, cardamom and cinnamon; sprinkle evenly over bread. Starting with a long edge, roll up bread, jelly-roll fashion; as you roll, tuck the blueberries in if they pop out. Press the dough together at the long edge once the dough is rolled. Cut into 8 even slices. Place in prepared baking dish with a cut side up; there will be a fair amount of space between the rolls. If some of the berries or nuts fall out, tuck them into the spirals. Cover with plastic wrap and let rise at room temperature for about an hour.

Near the end of the rising time, heat oven to 350°F. Uncover rolls. Bake until cooked through, 35 to 40 minutes; cover dish with foil during the last 10 minutes of baking if rolls are browning too quickly. Remove from oven, and remove foil if used. Let rolls cool for about 5 minutes, then cover with foil, bringing it down the sides of the dish. Place a baking sheet over the dish, and (using potholders) quickly but carefully flip everything over together. Remove the baking dish. Let cool at least 15 minutes before eating; best served warm and fresh.

 This recipe was developed for use with wild blueberries, which are much smaller than domestic blueberries. If domestic blueberries are substituted, the rolls have big gaps because the berries are too large!

Blueberry-Maple Breakfast Casserole 6 to 8 servings

A little preparation the night before lets you put a wonderful, warm breakfast together with ease. The maple syrup is a perfect complement to the blueberries.

1 loaf (1 pound) French bread, cut into ½-inch cubes

8 ounces cream cheese, cut into ½-inch cubes (reduced-fat works fine)

1 to 1½ cups fresh or previously frozen blueberries (4½ to 7 ounces)

8 eggs

2½ cups whole milk

½ cup real maple syrup

½ teaspoon salt

Spray 9x13-inch baking dish with nonstick spray. Distribute half of the bread cubes in the dish. Top with cream cheese cubes and blueberries, distributing evenly; top with remaining bread cubes. In large mixing bowl, beat together eggs, milk, syrup and salt until smooth. Pour evenly over bread. Cover and refrigerate overnight.

The next morning, heat oven to 350°F. Uncover dish; bake until top is golden brown and center is set, 35 to 45 minutes. Let stand 10 minutes before serving.

Other recipes in this book featuring blueberries and huckleberries:
> Refrigerator Cookies with Dried Berries, pg. 15
> Overnight Multi-Grain Cereal with Fruit and Nuts, pg. 56
> Serviceberry or Blueberry Freezer Jam, pg. 154
> Fruits of the Forest Pie, pg. 170
> Dehydrating Wild Berries and Fruits, pgs. 182–184
> Wild Berry or Fruit Leather, pg. 184
> As a substitute in Blackberry-Apple Crisp, pg. 21
> As a substitute in Individual Currant Cheesecakes, pg. 55
> As a substitute in Serviceberry Pudding Cake, pg. 153
> As a variation in Persimmon Smoothie, pg. 131

Quick ideas for using blueberries and huckleberries:
> Use fresh, wild blueberries or huckleberries in any recipe you
> have that calls for fresh blueberries.

CHERRIES: PIN, SWEET, SOUR, BLACK and SAND CHERRIES; CHOKECHERRIES
(Prunus pensylvanica, P. avium, P. cerasus, P. serotina, P. pumila; P. virginiana)

Wild cherries are tart but delicious; quality varies from tree to tree, but juice from all of them makes an exceptional, sparkling jelly. The flesh of pin cherries, chokecherries and black cherries is thin in proportion to the pits; sweet cherries, sour cherries and sand cherries are meatier, and can be pitted with a regular cherry pitter to make pie or other baked goods.

Black cherries are the most difficult to harvest, because the fruit is out of reach in the tall trees; sand cherries are the easiest, as they are a low shrub that bears heavily. Pin cherry, sweet cherry and sour cherry

Don't crush the pits of any of these fruits during cooking or straining. Cherry pits contain small amounts of a cyanide-forming compound that can cause illness if eaten in large quantities.

trees bear a lot of fruit, but it's tough to beat the birds to them; however, the fruit hangs low and a good deal can be gathered from the ground—if you're there at the right time. Chokecherries are easy to pick because the plants are lower-growing and produce plentiful fruit; also, the fruit grows in long clusters so it's easy to pull off a big handful rather than picking one fruit at a time.

Juice and purée prepared from all six species of cherries listed here is interchangeable, so all recipes in this section simply call for wild cherry juice, rather than listing all six species in each recipe. The only recipes that are not interchangeable are Duck Breast with Cherries (pg. 40) and Classic Cherry Pie (pg. 43), which really do need to be made with the large, fleshy cherries listed in the recipes—unless you have the patience to remove the pits from a gallon of one of the smaller, less-meaty cherries.

To prepare purée or juice, measure the fruit and place in a non-aluminum pot. For purée, add 1 cup water per quart of fruit; for juice, add 2 cups water per quart of fruit. Heat to boiling, then reduce the heat; cover and simmer for about 30 minutes, gently crushing the fruit with a potato masher near the end of cooking. **For purée,** process the cooked fruit through a cone-shaped colander or food mill, then discard the pits. **For juice,** transfer the mixture to a strainer lined with doubled, dampened cheesecloth and let it drip for 30 minutes; if you're making jelly, don't squeeze the fruit or the jelly will be cloudy. After the clear liquid has dripped away, set it aside and squeeze the fruit into a different container; you can use this slightly cloudy juice as a beverage or for cooking. Processed this way, a quart of fruit will yield about 1 cup of purée (slightly more for sweet, sour and sand cherries), or about 1½ cups juice.

Cherry Wigglers

These gelatin squares are firm enough to be carried in a lunchbox for several hours without melting in all but the hottest weather.

1³/₄ cups wild cherry juice, divided

2 envelopes unflavored gelatin

½ cup sugar

Spray an 8-inch-square baking dish with nonstick spray; set aside. Place ½ cup of the cherry juice in a small bowl; sprinkle gelatin on top and set aside. In non-aluminum saucepan, combine remaining 1¼ cups cherry juice and the sugar. Heat to boiling over medium-high heat and cook, stirring constantly, until mixture boils and sugar dissolves, about 3 minutes. Scrape gelatin mixture into saucepan; stir until the gelatin dissolves. Remove from heat and cool for about 5 minutes, then pour into prepared dish. Let cool at room temperature for about 15 minutes, then cover with plastic wrap, pressing the wrap against the surface of the mixture. Refrigerate until firm, about 3 hours. Cut into long, skinny fingers or 1-inch squares, as you prefer; store in the refrigerator in a tightly sealed plastic container with plastic wrap between the layers.

Wild Cherry Jelly

2½ cups wild cherry juice

2 tablespoons lemon juice

Two-thirds of a 1.75-ounce box powdered pectin

½ teaspoon butter, optional (helps reduce foaming)

2³/₄ cups sugar

Prepare and process as directed in Jelly Instructions (using pectin), pg. 178.

Cherry Barbecue Sauce

This works well with just about any grilled meat, but is particularly good on game such as duck and goose.

1¼ pounds whole wild cherries, stems removed

⅓ cup orange juice

¼ cup chopped shallot

1 tablespoon minced fresh gingerroot

½ teaspoon ground cumin

½ teaspoon freshly ground black pepper

1 small hot red pepper, stem and seeds removed

2 tablespoons tomato paste

2 tablespoons white wine vinegar

¾ teaspoon salt

In heavy-bottomed non-aluminum saucepan, combine cherries, orange juice, shallot, gingerroot, cumin, black pepper and hot pepper. Heat to boiling over medium heat, then cook, stirring occasionally, until most of the liquid has cooked away, about 20 minutes. Remove from heat and cool slightly, then process through food mill. Transfer purée to smaller heavy-bottomed non-aluminum saucepan; add tomato paste, vinegar and salt. Simmer over medium-low heat for 20 minutes, stirring occasionally; if sauce is thinner than you like, increase heat slightly and cook until reduced as much as you like.

If a recipe calls for a small quantity of tomato paste, you can freeze the rest of the can in small portions for future use. Drop the extra paste, in 1-tablespoon mounds, onto a piece of waxed paper set on top of a plate. Freeze until solid, then roll up the waxed paper with the tomato mounds, and store in a freezer container. Next time you need a tablespoon of tomato paste, simply unroll the waxed paper and peel off a tablespoon; it will thaw quickly, and be ready to use in a jiffy.

Duck Breast with Cherries

2 servings; easily increased

Slow roasting renders much of the duck fat out, leaving moist, tender meat and firm, golden skin. The skin is not super-crispy; depending on individual taste, it may be eaten or cut off.

2 boneless, skin-on Pekin duck breast halves (6½ to 7½ ounces each)

Garlic salt, seasoned salt or plain salt and pepper

1 medium onion

1 cup fresh or previously frozen pitted sour, sweet or sand cherry halves, with any juices collected during pitting or thawing

1 tablespoon balsamic vinegar

1 tablespoon honey

½ teaspoon dried thyme leaves

1 cup chicken broth

2 teaspoons cornstarch

Heat oven to 275°F. Prick duck skin all over with a sharp roasting fork or a very sharp paring knife. Sprinkle duck breast halves on both sides with the seasoning of your choice. Place breast halves together with skin sides out; tie snugly but not too tightly with 3 pieces of kitchen twine. Place breasts on roasting rack in shallow pan so one half is facing up and the other is facing down. Roast for 3 hours, turning over each hour and pricking skin each time. After 3 hours, spoon out and reserve 1 tablespoon of the rendered fat from the roasting pan; turn and prick skin again and continue roasting for another hour.

While breasts continue to roast, prepare the cherry sauce: Cut onion in half from top to bottom; reserve one half for another use. Cut remaining half crosswise into 2 pieces; cut out and discard root end. Slice the onion pieces vertically into slivers about ¼ inch wide. Heat the 1 tablespoon of duck fat in a medium skillet over medium heat until warm. Add onion; reduce heat to medium-low and cook, stirring occasionally, until caramelized, 15 to 20 minutes (if onions are browning too quickly, reduce heat to low). Add cherries and juice. Cook over medium-low heat, stirring frequently, for 5 minutes; if the mixture is still juicy, cook until fairly dry. Add balsamic vinegar, honey and thyme; cook until liquid has mostly cooked away and mixture is getting sticky, 3 to 5 minutes longer. In small bowl, blend together chicken broth and cornstarch; add to skillet with cherry mixture. Increase heat to medium and cook, stirring frequently, for 5 minutes; mixture should be thickened and bubbly. Transfer mixture to a small casserole; cover and set aside.

After the 4th hour of roasting, cut off the strings from the duck breasts and place breasts, skin side down, in the casserole on top of the cherry mixture. Flip the breast pieces so the skin side is up. Return to oven and roast for 15 minutes longer. Serve duck breasts with the sauce.

Wild Cherry Zabaglione

This light, fluffy dessert is an adaptation of zabaglione (zah-bye-LYOH-neh), a classic Italian dessert which is typically made with Marsala or other sweet wine. Serve it with shortbread cookies, or topped with fresh fruit such as raspberries.

1 cup whipping cream

2 tablespoons plus ⅓ cup sugar, divided

½ teaspoon vanilla extract

5 egg yolks

⅓ cup wild cherry juice

In large mixing bowl, combine cream, 2 tablespoons sugar and the vanilla. Beat with electric mixer until stiff. Refrigerate until needed.

Add 2 inches of water to the bottom of a double boiler that has a large top half; heat over medium heat until simmering. In top half of double boiler, combine egg yolks and remaining ⅓ cup sugar. Beat with electric hand mixer until fluffy and light-colored. Add cherry juice; beat with mixer until well combined. Place top half of double boiler over the bottom half so the egg mixture in the top half will be heated by the simmering water in the bottom half. Cook, beating constantly with electric mixer, until mixture is thick and holds soft peaks, 8 to 10 minutes. Remove top half of double boiler and place on a heat-proof surface; continue beating for 3 or 4 minutes. Let stand until completely cool, about 10 minutes. Add to mixing bowl with whipped cream, gently folding together with rubber spatula. Refrigerate for 30 minutes, or as long as 2 hours. Serve in parfait glasses.

Tip: If you have leftovers, transfer them to a freezer-safe container and freeze for at least 8 hours. The frozen zabaglione becomes an airy, delicious ice cream.

No Double Boiler?

If a recipe calls for use of a double boiler, but you don't have one, you can use a large stainless-steel bowl and a saucepan. Heat a few inches of water in the saucepan until simmering. Put the mixture to be cooked in the stainless-steel bowl, then set it on top of the saucepan and proceed as directed.

Homemade Cherry Cordial

The black cherry is sometimes called rum or whisky cherry because it was often used in the past to make a flavored liqueur. Here's a version of that for you to try.

2 cups whole wild cherries

1½ cups vodka

1½ cups brandy

2 strips orange zest, each about ½ inch wide and 1 inch long (colored rind only, with none of the white pith)

4 whole cloves

⅓ cup sugar

⅓ cup water

½ teaspoon glycerin (from the drugstore)

Sterilize a 1-quart canning jar, lid and band as directed on pg. 185. In large bowl, gently crush cherries with a potato masher; pick out and discard pits, squeezing over the bowl to extract any flesh or juice. Transfer cherries and juice to sterilized jar. Add vodka, brandy, orange zest and cloves. Seal jar with sterilized lid and shake well. Set in a cool, dark spot for 4 weeks, shaking occasionally.

At the end of 4 weeks, strain mixture through cheesecloth-lined strainer into a clean bowl; press on the cherries to extract the liquid. Discard the solids. Line a funnel with a paper coffee filter. Strain liquid into a clean, sterilized 1-quart canning jar; set aside.

In small saucepan, combine sugar and water. Heat over medium-low heat, stirring frequently, until sugar dissolves and liquid is clear. Remove from heat; set aside until completely cool. Strain syrup through a clean coffee filter into the jar with the cordial. Add glycerin; seal jar and shake to blend. Let stand, tightly sealed, for 2 or 3 days before serving; store in a cool, dark place for up to 3 months.

Zesting Citrus Fruits

The "zest" is the colored part of the rind only, with none of the bitter white pith. Always wash the fruit well before zesting.

To make zest strips, use a very sharp knife to cut off the colored part of the rind, being careful to avoid getting any of the white pith.

To make grated zest, the best tool is a microplane grater; this rasp-like tool looks like it belongs in a woodworker's shop, but it really is superior for grating zest. Hold the grater over a small bowl with the teeth facing up, and draw the fruit over the teeth. When you start to see the lighter part of the rind, rotate the fruit and grate in a fresh spot. If you don't have a microplane grater, use the fine holes on a box grater, or a porcelain ginger grater.

Wild Cherry-Lemonade Sparkler

This tangy, refreshing beverage goes down well when the mercury heads skyward.

1½ cups wild cherry juice

¾ cup freshly squeezed lemon juice

½ cup sugar, or to taste

1 can (12 ounces) lime-flavored carbonated water

In serving pitcher, combine cherry juice, lemon juice and sugar; stir to dissolve sugar. Add carbonated water; pour over ice in tall glasses. Note: If you don't want to serve all of the sparkler at once, mix the cherry juice, lemon juice and sugar first, then add to sparkling water as each drink is served.

Classic Cherry Pie

2½ cups pitted sour, sweet or sand cherries, plus juice that collects during pitting or thawing

⅓ cup white sugar

⅓ cup (packed) dark brown sugar

3 tablespoons minute tapioca

⅛ teaspoon almond extract, optional

Ready-to-use pastry for single-crust pie

1½ tablespoons butter, cut into small pieces

Heat oven to 425°F. In mixing bowl, combine cherries, juices from pitting, white and brown sugars, tapioca and almond extract. Stir well; let stand for 15 minutes. Meanwhile, line pie plate with pastry and flute edges decoratively; set aside until needed.

When cherries have rested for 15 minutes, scrape into prepared pie plate. Dot with butter. Place on baking sheet (to catch drips) and bake for 10 minutes; reduce heat to 350°F and bake until filling thickens and bubbles and crust is golden brown, about 30 minutes longer. Serve warm or at room temperature.

 Pit the cherries over a mixing bowl to collect all the precious juice.

Pumpkin Tart with Cherry Glaze

1 pie (6 to 8 servings)

Cherry juice is particularly good with pumpkin pie; the tartness cuts through the richness of the pie filling very well, and the color is lovely.

1 can (15 ounces) pumpkin

8 ounces cream cheese, softened

2 eggs

¾ cup sugar

1 teaspoon rum extract or vanilla extract, optional

1 teaspoon cinnamon

½ teaspoon ground ginger

¼ teaspoon allspice

**1 pre-baked pie crust, lightly golden
(see "Blind Baking Pie Crusts," pg. 61)**

3 cups cherry juice

2 tablespoons cornstarch mixed with 2 tablespoons cold water

Heat oven to 350°F. Combine pumpkin and cream cheese in large mixing bowl. Beat with electric mixer until smooth. Add eggs, sugar, extract, cinnamon, ginger and allspice; beat until smooth. Scrape into pre-baked crust, smoothing top. Bake until set, 45 to 60 minutes. Remove from oven and set aside until cool.

While tart is cooling, prepare glaze. Boil cherry juice until reduced to 2 cups (see "Reducing Liquid" on pg. 45). Stir in cornstarch mixture. Cook, stirring constantly, until thickened and bubbly. Remove from heat; set aside to cool slightly. Pour cooled mixture over tart, spreading and smoothing with back of spoon. Serve at room temperature; refrigerate leftovers.

Substitutions: Use elderberry or red currant juice in place of the cherry juice; darker juices like these look best with the pie.

Reducing Liquid

When a recipe calls for reducing liquid to a particular volume, it's hard to judge without measuring. Here's a better way. Before you start, measure water in the amount called for after reducing (so if the recipe says to boil 3 cups down to 1 cup, measure 1 cup of water). Place the water in the pan you'll be using, then stand a chopstick in the water. Use a knife to make a small dent in the chopstick at the water level, then discard the water and add the liquid to be reduced. When you think the liquid is getting close to the proper reduction, check it by standing the chopstick in the pan.

Easy Cherry Applesauce

About 2½ cups

This fast and easy applesauce is cooked in the microwave. Cherry pureé provides a lovely color, and a delightfully tangy flavor.

3 cups sliced apples (peeled, cored and sliced before measuring)

½ cup sugar, or as needed

⅔ cup wild cherry purée

½ teaspoon cinnamon

¼ teaspoon nutmeg

A good pinch of ground cardamom

Combine all ingredients in microwave-safe mixing bowl. Cover with waxed paper. Microwave on high power for 10 minutes or until apples are soft, stirring once halfway through. Cool apple mixture slightly, then mash to desired consistency with potato masher. Taste, and add additional sugar if necessary (stir the sugar into the warm sauce, and heat briefly in the microwave to incorporate the sugar). Serve warm or chilled.

Use Fireside, McIntosh, Granny Smith or other cooking apples; if you have a windfall of large crabapples, you can use them, but it's a lot of work to peel and core 3 cups of crabapples! Wild apples, of course, will work great in place of domestic apples.

Other recipes in this book featuring wild cherries:
Wild Grape-Black Cherry Wine, pg. 72
Six Recipes Using Wild Fruit Juice or Syrup, pgs. 172–176
Wild Berry or Fruit Syrup, pg. 177
Wild Berry or Fruit Leather, pg. 184
As a substitute in Spicy Plum Chutney, pg. 160
As a variation in Elderberry Meringue Pie, pg. 60
As a variation in Fruit Terrine with Elderberry Gel, pg. 62

CHOKEBERRIES or ARONIA *(Aronia melanocarpa)*

Most wild-foods books sold in the United States don't even mention chokeberries. They're much more common in central and eastern Europe, where they typically go by the more flattering name aronia. The juice is used as a beverage, and the fruits are combined with apples to make wine. Black chokeberries are the most common, but purple (*A. prunifolia*) and red (*A. arbutifolia*) chokeberries also grow in our area; the fruits can be used in the same way as black chokeberries.

Aronia juice is considered a health food, because the fruits are rich in anthocyanins, a phytonutrient that may lower blood pressure and protect against circulatory problems caused by diabetes.

Unlike chokecherries and many other fall fruits, chokeberries contain no inedible stone or large, annoying seeds. They grow in abundance on the shrubs, so it's easy to gather a good quantity. Chokeberries have a sweet flavor, but the flesh has an acrid quality that will leave your mouth feeling dry, similar to the effect of eating an underripe apple or a raw cranberry. The juice makes an excellent jelly or syrup, with no acrid feeling at all.

To prepare purée or juice, measure the chokeberries. Chop coarsely in a food processor (the fruit will stain any white parts of the processor, by the way), and place in a non-aluminum pot. For purée, add 1 cup water per quart of fruit (measured before chopping); for juice, add 2½ cups water per quart of fruit. Heat to boiling, then reduce the heat; cover and simmer for about 20 minutes. **For purée,** process the cooked fruit in the food processor again, until it is the desired texture. **For juice,** transfer the mixture to a strainer lined with doubled, dampened cheesecloth. Rinse the cooking pot with 1 cup of water, and pour that into the strainer with the other fruit. Let it drip for 30 minutes, then gently squeeze the cheesecloth bundle to extract more juice (your hands will turn purple, and remain that way for a day or two). Processed this way, a quart of chokeberries will yield about 2 cups of very dark pulp, or about 3 cups of rich, purplish-black juice; if your yield of juice is less, add water to make up the difference. Chokeberries may be frozen by following the instructions for blueberries on pg. 28.

Aronia Jelly

4 half-pints

2⅓ cups chokeberry juice

2 tablespoons lemon juice

Two-thirds of a 1.75-ounce box powdered pectin

½ teaspoon butter, optional (helps reduce foaming)

2½ cups sugar

Prepare and process as directed in Jelly Instructions (using pectin), pg. 178.

Chokeberry-Cornmeal Cake

The topping on this rustic cake is similar to that on caramel rolls—except it's dark purple! This cake is best on the day it's made; the caramelized topping gets soft overnight.

Topping:

3 tablespoons butter

¾ cup (packed) brown sugar

1¼ cups fresh or previously frozen chokeberries (about 6¼ ounces)

½ cup (1 stick) butter, softened

¾ cup white sugar

2 eggs

⅓ cup sour cream

1 teaspoon vanilla extract

1 cup all-purpose flour

½ cup cornmeal

1½ teaspoons baking powder

¼ teaspoon salt

Cut a square of kitchen parchment to fit the bottom of an 8-inch-square baking dish. Spray dish with nonstick spray; place parchment in bottom, smoothing in place. Set aside. Make the topping: In small saucepan, melt butter over medium heat. Add brown sugar and cook, stirring constantly, until smooth. Add chokeberries; increase heat to medium-high and cook, stirring occasionally, until mixture comes to a boil. Cook, stirring frequently, for about 3 minutes. Remove from heat and set aside until cool. Heat oven to 350°F.

In large mixing bowl, beat butter with electric mixer until smooth and light. Add white sugar; beat until fluffy. Add eggs one at a time, beating after each addition. Add sour cream and vanilla; beat well. Place wire-mesh strainer over the mixing bowl. Add flour, cornmeal, baking powder and salt; shake to sift into bowl. Fold in with rubber spatula until just moistened. Pour cooled berry mixture into prepared pan. Spoon batter evenly into baking dish over berry mixture, spreading gently; it will not be flat but that's okay. Bake until top is light brown and springs back when touched lightly, 40 to 50 minutes. Transfer pan to wire rack and let cool for 10 minutes, then run a table knife around the edges to loosen. Place a flat platter (or small sheet pan) on top of the pan and carefully invert the two together; remove baking dish. Remove parchment. Let cool for at least 30 minutes before serving; serve warm or at room temperature.

Pear and Chokeberry Mincemeat

1 quart

Use this filling to make pie (pg. 49), or warm it up and serve over ice cream or pound cake.

2 pounds ripe but firm Anjou, Bartlett or other pears (or about 2½ pounds wild pears), peeled, quartered and cored, then cut into thirds

⅔ cup fresh or previously frozen chokeberries (about 4 ounces)

2 tablespoons freshly squeezed lemon juice

⅔ cup sugar

¾ cup water, divided

2 teaspoons corn syrup

½ cup golden raisins

¼ cup dried cranberries (craisins)

½ teaspoon cinnamon

½ teaspoon allspice

¼ teaspoon nutmeg

¼ teaspoon salt

¾ cup chopped pecans, butternuts or hickory nuts (medium-fine)

2 tablespoons rum or brandy, or ½ teaspoon rum extract

2 tablespoons unsalted butter

In food processor, combine pears, chokeberries and lemon juice; chop until pears are coarse, with pieces no larger than ½ inch (or, chop fruits by hand, sprinkling afterwards with lemon juice). Set aside.

In heavy-bottomed non-aluminum 4-quart saucepan, stir sugar, ¼ cup water and the corn syrup together. Cook over medium heat, stirring constantly with a wooden spoon, until sugar dissolves and mixture comes to a boil. Continue to cook, stirring occasionally, until mixture turns golden, about 7 minutes; watch carefully, as the syrup colors rapidly and it's easy to burn it. Remove pan from heat and carefully add the remaining ½ cup water, avoiding the steam that will rise. The syrup will harden when the water is added. Return to medium heat and cook, stirring constantly, until the hardened syrup dissolves. Add pear mixture, raisins, cranberries, cinnamon, allspice, nutmeg and salt. Adjust heat so mixture boils gently. Cook, stirring frequently, until thickened, 45 to 50 minutes.

Add nuts, rum and butter. Cook, stirring frequently, for about 5 minutes. If canning, process immediately as described below; otherwise, cool completely before storing in refrigerator or freezing. To can: Follow canning instructions on pg. 185. Pack hot mincemeat into hot pint jars. Process in boiling-water bath for 20 minutes.

Pear and Chokeberry Mincemeat Pie   1 pie (6 to 8 servings)

For a holiday treat, serve this pie warm with a scoop of vanilla ice cream, or a big dollop of lightly sweetened whipped cream.

Ready-to-use pastry for double-crust pie

3½ to 4 cups Pear and Chokeberry Mincemeat (pg. 48)

1½ teaspoons unsalted butter, cut into small pieces

1 egg yolk, beaten with 1 tablespoon cold water

Fit one of the pastries into an ungreased pie plate. Trim edges, leaving ¾ inch overhang. Cover and chill pie crust and remaining pastry dough for 30 minutes.

When pastry has chilled, heat oven to 425°F. Spoon mincemeat into prepared crust; the crust should be comfortably full but not over the edge. Dot top with butter. Moisten edges of pastry in pie plate, then top with second pastry, or make a lattice top as described on pg. 171. Seal, trim and flute edges. Brush top crust with egg wash; if you've used a plain top crust rather than a lattice, cut inch-long slits in the crust in 6 to 8 places for ventilation. Place pie on baking sheet (to catch drips) and bake in center of oven until crust is golden and filling bubbles through vents or lattices, about 25 minutes. Cool to warm room temperature before serving; best served on the day it is made.

 Don't worry if you can't make this pie the same day you make the chokeberry mincemeat. The mincemeat will keep for a week in the refrigerator, and the flavor actually improves after a day or two.

Other recipes in this book featuring chokeberries:
Six Recipes Using Wild Fruit Juice or Syrup, pgs. 172–176
Wild Berry or Fruit Syrup, pg. 177
Wild Berry or Fruit Leather, pg. 184

Quick ideas for using chokeberries:
If you're a winemaker, experiment with a chokeberry-apple wine; it's often sold in Europe and is reportedly delicious.
Chokeberry juice can be used in any recipe calling for chokecherry, wild cherry or elderberry juice.

CRANBERRIES *(Vaccinium macrocarpon, V. oxycoccus)*

Two varieties of wild cranberry—large and small—are found in our region; other than size differences, they are quite similar to each other and to commercially grown cranberries. Like the commercial variety, wild cranberries can be eaten raw, but they are quite tart. They are more commonly cooked, or ground and enhanced with orange juice and sugar to make a relish.

Wild cranberries can be used exactly as you would use purchased cranberries, although fruits of the wild species are typically a bit smaller.

To prepare cranberry juice, measure the fruit. Chop coarsely in a food processor, and place in a non-aluminum pot. Add 2½ cups water per quart of fruit. Heat to boiling, then reduce the heat; cover and simmer for about 10 minutes. Transfer the mixture to a strainer lined with doubled, dampened cheesecloth and let it drip for 30 minutes; if you're making jelly, don't squeeze the fruit or the jelly will be cloudy. After the clear liquid has dripped away, set it aside and squeeze the fruit into a different container; you can use this slightly cloudy juice as a beverage or for cooking. Processed this way, a quart of fruit will yield about 3 cups of bright red juice.

Cranberries freeze well; simply spread them out on a baking sheet and freeze overnight, then pack into freezer-weight plastic bags or other containers. They can be dehydrated and eaten out of hand as a snack; home-dehydrated fruits can also be used in recipes calling for craisins.

Cranberry Jelly
5 half-pints

3 cups cranberry juice

2 tablespoons lemon juice

Half of a 1.75-ounce box powdered pectin

½ teaspoon butter, optional (helps reduce foaming)

3½ cups sugar

Prepare and process as directed in Jelly Instructions (using pectin), pg. 178.

Variation: If you want a more firm jelly that can be sliced rather than spread, use 2 cups cranberry juice, 2 tablespoons lemon juice, a 3-ounce pouch liquid pectin and 3 cups sugar. Prepare and process as above, pouring the cooked jelly into 2 wide-mouth one-pint canning jars before processing. When ready to serve, place the jar in a pot of very hot water (enough to come up to the level of jelly in the jar); let stand for about 5 minutes. Slide the jelly out onto a plate; if it resists, run a table knife around the edges. Cut into ¼-inch-thick slices to serve alongside poultry, pork or venison.

Fresh Cranberry Relish

About 1½ cups

This uncooked relish has a wonderful sweet and tangy taste. Serve it in a glass bowl to show off the lovely color.

1 navel orange, well washed

1 cup sugar

1 cup fresh cranberries

1 Granny Smith or other tart apple

Use a sharp paring knife to remove the zest (colored rind only, with none of the white pith) from half of the orange, cutting the zest in strips. Add to food processor, along with sugar. Process until zest is finely chopped. Peel orange, and divide into halves; wrap and refrigerate one half for other uses. Divide remaining orange half into sections and remove any seeds. Add orange sections and cranberries to food processor. Peel and core the apple, then cut into 1-inch chunks. Add to food processor. Pulse on-and-off in very short bursts, scraping down the sides of the workbowl, until mixture is chopped to a medium consistency; don't over-process. Transfer to a glass or ceramic bowl; let stand at room temperature for an hour to allow sugar to dissolve and flavors to blend.

Variation: Add ¼ cup pecan halves to the fruit before processing.

 My mother-in-law tells of making fresh cranberry relish when she was growing up on a farm in western Minnesota. They used a hand-cranked meat grinder to chop the fruit. If you have a meat grinder, give it a try with this recipe (use the medium plate); the texture is very nice.

Other recipes in this book featuring cranberries:
Pear and Chokeberry Mincemeat, pg. 48
Overnight Multi-Grain Cereal with Fruit and Nuts, pg. 56
Spicy Gooseberry-Apple Crisp, pg. 66
Muscadine Bars, pg. 105
Six Recipes Using Wild Fruit Juice or Syrup, pgs. 172–176
Wild Berry or Fruit Syrup, pg. 177
Dehydrating Wild Berries and Fruits, pgs. 182–184

Quick ideas for using cranberries:
Use in any recipe that calls for commercial cranberries.
Sweeten the juice to taste, and serve as a breakfast or appetizer drink; it's also good when blended with apple or other juice.

CURRANTS *(Ribes spp.)*

Several varieties of currant are found in our area; all can be used in the same way, although their taste varies quite a bit. They can be eaten raw, although most are fairly tart. When properly prepared, however, their tartness accents other flavors; they work well in savory dishes as well as sweet. Flavor varies from plant to plant; before harvesting a large quantity, taste them to be sure they will work for your uses. Red currants tend to be sweeter than black ones, but this is not a hard-and-fast rule.

Ripe currants retain their quality even if they are left on the plant for a week or more; I usually find, however, that birds and other critters have beaten me to the berries once they're ripe, so don't wait too long to harvest them.

Currants grow in racemes, long clusters containing multiple fruits. Snip off the entire cluster rather than trying to pick the fruits off individually, unless the fruits have ripened unevenly. At home, wash the clusters and pull individual berries off the stemlets. If you're using them whole for baking or other dishes, also remove the dried flower remnant at the bottom; if you're making juice, don't bother with this step. Currants have small seeds that are noticeable but not objectionable; however, some people prefer to cook the fruit and strain it to remove the seeds.

To prepare currant juice, measure the fruit and place in a non-aluminum pot. Add ½ cup water per quart of fruit. Gently crush the fruit with a potato masher to start the juices flowing. Heat to boiling, then reduce the heat; cover and simmer for about 10 minutes. Transfer the mixture to a strainer lined with doubled, dampened cheesecloth and let it drip for 30 minutes; if you're making jelly, don't squeeze the fruit or the jelly will be cloudy. After the clear liquid has dripped away, set it aside and squeeze the fruit into a different container; you can use this slightly cloudy juice as a beverage or for cooking. Processed this way, a quart of fruit will yield about 2 cups juice.

Currants freeze well. Wash them and remove the blossom remnant, then either spread in a single layer on a baking sheet and freeze overnight, or pack into containers in measured amounts and freeze. If you've frozen them on a baking sheet, pack the frozen berries into containers and store in the freezer; you can measure out what you need and return the rest to the freezer. Currants are also a good choice for drying; note that the fruit sold in the store as "dried currants" is actually a dried grape, so your home-dried currants will be quite different.

Currant-Basil Sauce

About ½ cup sauce, enough for 4 servings

Basil adds a sweet, grassy note to the tangy currants in this savory sauce. Serve it over grilled or poached fish such as salmon or trout; it's also delicious with grilled pork tenderloin or chops.

2 tablespoons finely chopped shallots

1 teaspoon olive oil

¼ cup seasoned rice vinegar

2 tablespoons dry, fruity red wine, such as Tempranillo or Beaujolais

2 tablespoons finely chopped fresh basil leaves

1 teaspoon sugar

¾ cup fresh red or black currants (about 4 ounces)

1 tablespoon unsalted butter

Salt and pepper

In small skillet, sauté shallots in oil over medium heat for about 3 minutes. Stir in vinegar, wine, basil and sugar. Cook until liquid reduces by half, 3 to 5 minutes. Add currants; cook, stirring occasionally, until the mixture is saucy, about 5 minutes. Remove from heat; add butter and stir until melted. Season to taste with salt and pepper. Spoon warm sauce over prepared fish or pork.

Salted vs. Unsalted Butter

Many recipes in this book call specifically for unsalted butter. I have long believed that some creameries use fresher cream to make unsalted butter than that which is used for salted butter, because fresher cream is less likely to have "off" flavors, which salt helps cover in less-fresh, salted butter. Even if both types of butter are made from the exact same cream, unsalted butter has a fresher, cleaner taste than salted butter.

If a recipe calls for unsalted butter, you may substitute salted butter, but should reduce any added salt a bit to make up for the extra salt in the butter. If a recipe doesn't specifically call for salted or unsalted butter, feel free to use the type you have on hand; if you tend to like saltier food, then salted butter is a good choice, but if you're watching sodium intake, unsalted butter is a better option.

Red Currant and Blue Cheese Butter

About ½ cup, enough for 8 servings

This is outstanding when melted atop a freshly grilled steak; try it with grilled venison for an extra-special treat.

½ cup (1 stick) unsalted butter, softened

¼ cup red currants (about 1¼ ounces)

1 small clove garlic, pressed

4 ounces blue cheese, crumbled

In mixing bowl, combine butter, currants and garlic. Mash with a fork until well combined. Add blue cheese and mash lightly to combine; some of the blue cheese should retain its texture. Spoon mixture onto a piece of waxed paper, in a line about 8 inches long. Roll up the waxed paper tightly, forming a cylinder; twist the ends closed. Refrigerate for at least 2 hours, or as long as 5 days. To serve, slice off 1-inch-long pieces; place on hot steaks that are fresh from the grill or broiler.

For longer storage, wrap the butter roll in foil and freeze. It will keep for several months in the freezer; you can slice off what you need from the frozen roll and return it to the freezer.

Currant Jelly

4 half-pints

3 cups currant juice

Half of a 1.75-ounce box powdered pectin

½ teaspoon butter, optional (helps reduce foaming)

3¼ cups sugar

Prepare and process as directed in Jelly Instructions (using pectin), pg. 178.

Individual Currant Cheesecakes

Here's a fun recipe for picnics or parties—individual cheesecakes studded with colorful currants. The graham cracker crust adds nice texture.

1 tablespoon butter

6 squares graham crackers (about 1¾ ounces), finely crushed

1 package (8 ounces) cream cheese, softened

¼ cup sugar

1 egg

1 teaspoon vanilla extract

1 cup fresh red or black currants (about 5½ ounces)

You'll also need: 10 foil baking cups (cupcake liners made of foil)

Heat oven to 350°F. Use foil baking cups to line 10 standard-sized muffin cups. In small microwave-safe bowl, melt butter. Stir in crushed graham crackers. Divide evenly between baking cups (about 1 tablespoon per cup); set aside.

In mixing bowl, combine cream cheese and sugar. Beat with electric mixer until smooth. Add egg and vanilla; beat until well combined. Add currants; stir in gently with a spatula. Divide mixture evenly between prepared baking cups. Bake for about 30 minutes, or until just set and tops are beginning to turn golden brown. Cool to room temperature; refrigerate for at least 4 hours before serving.

Substitutions: Use serviceberries, blueberries or ripe gooseberries in place of the currants, or use a mix of these fruits. Frozen berries may also be used; defrost before using.

Overnight Multi-Grain Cereal with Fruit and Nuts

Bulk recipe

This is a wonderful mix to keep on hand. With just a few minutes' prep in the evening, you'll have hearty, cooked breakfast cereal in the morning—and no sticky pan to clean up!

¾ cup dried currants, cranberries or blueberries

⅔ cup chopped pecans

½ cup steel-cut (coarse) oatmeal

⅜ cup buckwheat groats

⅜ cup bulgur

¼ cup pepitas (toasted green pumpkin seeds)

¼ cup pearled barley

¼ cup soft wheat berries

2 tablespoons amaranth

Combine all ingredients in a large bowl; mix well with your hands. Store in a tightly sealed canister.

To prepare: The night before, measure ⅓ cup of the mixture per serving. For each serving, place ⅞ cup water and a pinch of salt in a saucepan or pot. Heat water to boiling. Add the measured mix; stir well. Return to boiling, then cover tightly and remove from the heat. Let stand at room temperature overnight. The next morning, the grains and fruit will be tender; heat on the stovetop or in the microwave, and serve with milk, syrup, butter, sugar or whatever you like. If you cook extra, you can keep it in the refrigerator for several days, heating a portion whenever you like.

The mix above is just a suggestion; feel free to alter the ingredients to suit your taste. Look for the grains and other specialty items at a health-food store, or in the bulk bins at co-ops and stores that specialize in natural or organic foods. Other options to consider: millet, spelt, farro, Kamut®, oat groats, flax seed, wheat germ, and any other dried fruit you like.

Currant Cordial

1 quart

Offer this delightful cordial to guests as a special after-dinner drink. It's also wonderfully warming to sip while sitting around the fireplace on a cold winter's night.

3 cups currant juice

½ cup sugar

1 cup brandy

2 whole cardamom pods

2 strips orange zest (colored rind only, with none of the white pith), each about ½ inch wide and 2 inches long

You'll need a glass bottle that holds at least 40 ounces to hold the cordial; juice is often sold in these types of bottles. Wash it very well, then fill it with boiling water and let stand for at least 5 minutes.

In non-aluminum saucepan, combine currant juice and sugar; heat to boiling over medium-high heat and cook, stirring constantly, until sugar dissolves. Remove from heat and set aside until cool. Drain water from the prepared glass bottle, then use a funnel to pour the juice into it. Add remaining ingredients. Seal tightly and place in a dark, cool cupboard to mellow for a few weeks before drinking.

 A cordial is similar to a liqueur, but with a lower alcohol content. If you make this cordial with red currant juice, it's a lovely garnet color; if you use black currant juice, it looks like blackberry brandy.

Other recipes in this book featuring currants:
Six Recipes Using Wild Fruit Juice or Syrup, pgs. 172–176
Wild Berry or Fruit Syrup, pg. 177
Dehydrating Wild Berries and Fruits, pgs. 182–184
As a substitute in Pumpkin Tart with Cherry Glaze, pg. 44

Quick ideas for using currants:
If the currants are sweet, serve them raw in a bowl topped with thick cream and lots of sugar.
Add dried currants to hot cereal when cooking. Delicious.

ELDERBERRIES, COMMON (Sambucus canadensis)

Elderberries have a somewhat musty flavor when sampled raw, but cooking improves the taste, especially when lemon juice is added. Don't taste more than one or two raw, though; many people get an upset stomach from raw elderberries. The seeds also cause digestive problems for some people; if you make an elderberry pie with whole berries, try just a small portion until you are sure you won't have a problem with the seeds.

Pick elderberries by snipping the entire fruit cluster off; place them in a bucket until you have as many as you need. The small stemlets that remain attached to the berries taste bad and can also cause digestive problems. The berries should be pulled off the stemlets soon after picking, because once the stemlets start to wilt, they are more difficult to remove. I rinse the clusters as soon as I get home, then just pull the berries off with my fingertips (which are soon stained purple). Some foragers prefer to place the clusters on a rimmed baking sheet that is propped up on one end, then use a fork to rake the berries off the clusters.

Flowers of the common elderberry can be steeped to make a tea, which is often recommended to relieve headaches. The flower cluster can also be battered and fried to make interesting fritters.

To prepare elderberry juice, measure the stemmed fruit and place in a non-aluminum pot. Add 1 cup water per quart of stemmed fruit. Heat to boiling, then reduce the heat; cover and simmer for about 5 minutes. Crush gently with a potato masher, then simmer for about 5 minutes longer. Transfer the mixture to a strainer lined with doubled, dampened cheesecloth and let it drip for 30 minutes; squeeze once or twice to extract more juice (elderberry juice is so dark that you won't have to worry about the jelly being cloudy if you squeeze the fruit). Processed this way, a quart of fruit will yield about 2 cups juice.

Whole elderberries freeze very well; place measured amounts of stemmed berries in freezer-weight plastic bags or plastic containers, label with the amount, and freeze. Elderberries are also easy to dry, and can sometimes be found in this form at wine-making supply stores. In addition to being used in winemaking, dried elderberries are used in baked goods, although if you want to try this, keep in mind that the seeds will still be in the dried fruit. To reconstitute dried elderberries, simply cover them generously with warm water and let stand until plumped up. A few reconstituted elderberries added to a batch of muffins, or to an apple pie, will make a delicious and different dessert. The soaking liquid can be added to other fruit juice for an interesting beverage.

Elderberry Liqueur

This lovely purple liqueur can be served straight in a cordial glass, or on the rocks.

2 cups stemmed fresh elderberries

2 cups water

¾ cup sugar

2 cups vodka

¼ cup freshly squeezed lemon juice

1 teaspoon anise seeds

You'll need a glass bottle that holds at least 40 ounces to hold the liqueur during its steeping period; juice is often sold in these types of bottles. Wash it very well, then fill it with boiling water and let stand for at least 5 minutes.

In blender or food processor, chop elderberries coarsely. In non-aluminum saucepan, combine water and sugar. Heat to boiling over medium-high heat, stirring constantly until sugar dissolves and mixture is clear. Add chopped elderberries; reduce heat to low and cook for 5 minutes, stirring occasionally. Remove from heat and set aside until cool. Drain water from glass bottle, then use a funnel to pour mixture into it. Add vodka, lemon juice and anise seeds. Seal tightly and place in a dark, cool cupboard for 2 to 3 weeks, shaking the bottle every day or two.

After steeping for 2 or 3 weeks, strain the mixture into another clean bottle through a strainer lined with a double layer of cheesecloth; discard mixture in cheesecloth. Refrigerate strained liquid for 8 hours or longer, to allow any sediment to settle. Pour clear liquid into a clean 1-quart bottle through a funnel lined with a paper coffee filter. For best quality, store in refrigerator.

 To make an elderberry martini, combine 2 parts elderberry liqueur with 1 part gin in an ice-filled cocktail shaker; shake and strain into a chilled martini glass. Garnish with a curl of lemon zest.

Elderberry Meringue Pie

1 pie (6 to 8 servings)

This pie looks so pretty, with the dark purple filling and fluffy meringue. It also looks like you spent all day slaving over it, but really, it's quite easy to make.

1 cup plus 1 tablespoon sugar

5 tablespoons cornstarch

⅛ teaspoon salt

1 cup elderberry juice

½ cup water

4 egg yolks

2 tablespoons butter

½ cup freshly squeezed lemon juice

**1 pre-baked pie crust, lightly golden
(see "Blind Baking Pie Crusts," pg. 61)**

<u>Meringue:</u>

4 egg whites*

½ teaspoon vanilla extract

¼ teaspoon cream of tartar

½ cup sugar

Heat oven to 350°F. In medium non-aluminum saucepan, stir sugar, cornstarch and salt together. Whisking constantly, stir in elderberry juice and water. Cook over medium-high heat, whisking constantly, until mixture boils; reduce heat to low and cook, whisking constantly, about 3 minutes longer. Remove from heat.

In small bowl, beat egg yolks lightly with a fork. Add ½ cup of the warm elderberry mixture to the egg yolks; beat with fork until smooth. Whisk egg yolk mixture into elderberry mixture. Return to medium-high heat and cook, whisking constantly, until thick, 3 to 4 minutes. Remove from heat. Add butter; whisk until dissolved. Add lemon juice; whisk until well blended. Scrape mixture into pre-baked pie crust; set aside while you prepare the meringue.

Prepare the meringue: In very clean mixing bowl, combine egg whites, vanilla and cream of tartar. Beat with electric mixer until soft peaks form. Gradually add sugar, beating continuously; continue beating until mixture is glossy and stiff peaks form. Spoon mixture over filling in crust, spreading all the way to the edges of the filling to seal to the crust;

use a spoon to pull some of the meringue up into peaks. Bake for 12 to 15 minutes, or until golden brown. Cool before serving.

*Use egg whites from pasteurized eggs if concerned about salmonella. You may also be able to purchase cartons of pasteurized egg whites, sold specifically for use in recipes such as meringue, at larger supermarkets.

Variation: Substitute juice from wild cherries or chokecherries for the elderberry juice; increase sugar to 1¼ cups. Or, substitute highbush cranberry juice for the elderberry juice; increase sugar to 1⅔ cups.

Blind Baking Pie Crusts
Sometimes, a recipe calls for a pre-baked pie crust. Here's how to make one. Place the rolled-out pastry dough into a pie plate; flute the edges decoratively. Place a large piece of foil inside, pressing it into the corners. Fill the foil with uncooked dry beans; if you do a lot of baking, you can also buy aluminum pie weights for this purpose at specialty cookware stores. Bake at 375°F for 10 minutes. Remove from oven. Carefully lift the foil by the corners, folding it in to contain the beans; place it in a mixing bowl and set it aside. Return the pie crust to the oven. For recipes that will get additional baking, bake until firm and very lightly golden, about 10 minutes more; for recipes that will get little or no additional baking, bake until golden brown, about 15 minutes more. Let crust cool before filling, or as directed in recipe.
The beans can no longer be used for bean recipes, but they can be saved for use when blind baking pies in the future; simply cool them completely, then transfer to a heavyweight plastic bag and store in the cupboard until you need them.

Elderberry Jelly   4 half-pints

For a delightful variation, also see Elderberry-Sumac Jelly on pg. 63.

2½ cups elderberry juice

3 tablespoons lemon juice

Two-thirds of a 1.75-ounce box powdered pectin

½ teaspoon butter, optional (helps reduce foaming)

2¾ cups sugar

Prepare and process as directed in Jelly Instructions (using pectin), pg. 178.

Fruit Terrine with Elderberry Gel

6 to 8 servings

This combines elderberry juice with fresh, purchased fruits for a truly lovely dessert—a clear gel glistening with fruits.

2 tablespoons cold water

2 tablespoons plain gelatin

1 cup elderberry juice

1 cup apple juice

½ cup sugar

1 cup cut-up peaches (fresh or previously frozen), cut into ½-inch pieces before measuring

1 cup fresh raspberries (wild or domestic)

1 cup whole, seedless green grapes (smaller grapes work best here)

A small amount of whipped cream for garnish, optional

Place cold water in a small bowl; sprinkle gelatin over the top. Let stand until gelatin softens, about 5 minutes. While gelatin is softening, in medium saucepan, combine elderberry juice, apple juice and sugar. Cook over medium heat, stirring constantly, until sugar dissolves, about 5 minutes. Remove from heat. Scrape softened gelatin into fruit juices; stir until gelatin is dissolved, 2 to 3 minutes. Cool to lukewarm.

While juice mixture is cooling, arrange peaches, raspberries and grapes in standard-sized glass loaf pan. Pour lukewarm fruit juice mixture over fruits; if any fruit is floating, press it down into the juice. Cover pan with plastic wrap and refrigerate until set, at least 3 hours; terrine can be prepared up to a day in advance.

To serve, run about 2 inches of hot water into the sink, then hold the pan in the sink so the water is level with the top of the gel; let stand in the hot water for about 15 seconds to loosen. (If it isn't loose along the sides, run a table knife between the gel and the pan.) Place a serving plate on top of the loaf pan and invert the two together, holding the plate and pan together tightly. Shake the pan slightly if necessary to release the terrine. Use a very sharp knife to slice crosswise into 6 to 8 pieces; top each serving with a small dollop of whipped cream, if you like.

Variation: Substitute juice from wild cherries or chokecherries for the elderberry juice. Increase sugar to ⅔ cup.

Elderberry-Sumac Jelly

4 half-pints

Elderberry jelly is delicious on its own, but sumac juice raises it to another level. This is one of the finest wild jellies you can make. The idea for this delightful combination comes from the late Euell Gibbons, in his book Stalking the Wild Asparagus.

3 cups stemless fresh elderberries, or 1 cup dried

2½ cups strained sumac juice (pg. 166)

Two-thirds of a 1.75-ounce box powdered pectin

½ teaspoon butter, optional (helps reduce foaming)

2¾ cups sugar

In non-aluminum saucepan, combine elderberries and sumac juice. Heat to a gentle boil. If using fresh elderberries, cook for 5 minutes, then crush gently with potato masher and cook for 5 minutes longer. If using dried elderberries, cook for 10 minutes, then remove from heat and let stand for 20 minutes.

Transfer the mixture to a strainer lined with doubled, dampened cheesecloth and let it drip for 30 minutes; squeeze once or twice to extract more juice. Measure the juice; add water if necessary to bring it up to 2½ cups. Prepare and process as directed in Jelly Instructions (using pectin), pg. 178.

Other recipes in this book featuring elderberries:
Wild Berry Vinegar, pg. 19
Six Recipes Using Wild Fruit Juice or Syrup, pgs. 172–176
Wild Berry or Fruit Syrup, pg. 177
Dehydrating Wild Berries and Fruits, pgs. 182–184
As a substitute in Pumpkin Tart with Cherry Glaze, pg. 44

Quick ideas for using elderberries:
Elderberry wine is often considered to be one of the best of the wild fruit wines, but it requires a lot of berries—and the stemlets need to be removed before you start. If you want to try making it, check out *Progressive Winemaking* by Peter Duncan and Bryan Acron.
Use the whole berries to make a pie, following any recipe you've got for blueberry pie; reconstituted dried berries are particularly good for pie. As noted on page 58, eat only a very small portion of this pie until you know you're not going to have a reaction to the seeds.

GOOSEBERRIES *(Ribes spp.)*

Three types of gooseberries grow in our area: Missouri, prickly and smooth. Fruits from these species taste about the same, so they all work for any gooseberry recipe. Gooseberries are unusual because the fruit can be used in its green stage as well as when fully ripe. They have a tart, refreshing flavor, somewhat reminiscent of rhubarb; ripe gooseberries are sweeter than green ones. Green gooseberries are rich in pectin, so they can be used to make jam without adding commercial pectin; they also make a good pie filling, because the pectin helps thicken the juices naturally.

Yes, those fierce-looking prickly gooseberries are edible! The spines are fairly soft, so picking them isn't painful (except for the thorns that grow on the stems). Cooking softens the prickles, making them unnoticeable.

When picking green gooseberries, choose those that are close to full size, about ⅜ inch across; they will still be firm, but will begin to appear slightly translucent around the edges. Taste one before picking a lot (unless you're picking prickly gooseberries, which are too spiny to taste raw). If the berry is hard and tastes acrid, the gooseberries are underripe; wait a week or so before picking. As summer progresses, you'll see gooseberries in all stages of ripeness on the plant at the same time, and you'll quickly get a feel for judging the correct stage.

Gooseberries grow abundantly on the plants, and you'll often find plants in small colonies, so it's easy to pick a good quantity. The work starts once you get them home, because you'll need to remove the stems and the "pigtail," a withered brown flower remnant at the base of the berry (if you're juicing the fruit, you don't need to remove the stems or tails). To clean green gooseberries, use a very sharp paring knife to slice off the stem and all parts of the pigtail. A knife works best on green gooseberries, which are firm enough to allow slicing. Once gooseberries ripen, the pressure of the knife and your fingertips tends to mangle the berries; sharp scissors work better (or pinch the stems and tails off with your fingernails).

To make gooseberry juice, place washed gooseberries in a small non-aluminum soup pot (you don't need to remove the stems or tails). Gently crush the fruit with a potato masher to start the flow of juice. Add ½ cup water per quart of gooseberries. Heat to boiling, then reduce the heat; cover and simmer for about 10 minutes. Transfer the mixture to a strainer lined with doubled, dampened cheesecloth and let it drip for 30 minutes; if you're making jelly, don't squeeze the fruit or the jelly will be cloudy. After the clear liquid has dripped away, set it aside and squeeze the fruit into a different container; you can use this slightly cloudy juice as a beverage or for cooking. Processed this way, a quart of gooseberries will yield about 2 cups of juice.

Gooseberries freeze well. Simply wash them and remove the stems and tails, then freeze in heavyweight plastic food-storage bags or tightly lidded plastic containers.

Green Gooseberry Pie

This is an old-time recipe, from back in the days when every farmhouse had a gooseberry pie cooling on the windowsill during "goosie season."

3½ cups green gooseberries (about 1¼ pounds)

1½ cups sugar

2 tablespoons minute tapioca

**½ teaspoon finely grated orange zest
(colored rind only, with none of the white pith)**

¼ teaspoon nutmeg

¼ teaspoon salt

Ready-to-use pastry for double-crust pie

1½ tablespoons unsalted butter, cut into small pieces

1 egg yolk, beaten with 1 tablespoon cold water

Heat oven to 375°F. In mixing bowl, combine gooseberries, sugar, tapioca, orange zest, nutmeg and salt. Stir gently until well mixed; set aside for 15 minutes. Meanwhile, fit one pastry into ungreased deep-dish pie plate. Scrape gooseberry mixture into pie plate. Dot with cut-up butter. Moisten edges of pastry in pie plate with a little cold water, then top with second pastry (for the most authentic farmhouse look, make a lattice-top pie; see below). Seal, trim and flute edges. Cut 6 to 8 inch-long slits in the crust. Place pie on baking sheet (to catch drips). Brush top with beaten egg. Bake until crust is golden and filling bubbles through slits, 35 to 40 minutes. Transfer to rack to cool; best served warm, the day it is made.

Ripe Gooseberry Jelly

3 cups gooseberry juice (prepared from ripe gooseberries)

One-third of a 1.75-ounce box powdered pectin

½ teaspoon butter, optional (helps reduce foaming)

3¼ cups sugar

Prepare and process as directed in Jelly Instructions (using pectin), pg. 178.

Spicy Gooseberry-Apple Crisp

Fruit mixture:

2 large Granny Smith or other tart cooking apples (about 1 pound), peeled, cored and cut into ½-inch chunks

2 cups fresh or previously frozen ripe gooseberries (about 12 ounces)

¾ cup (packed) brown sugar

½ cup dried cranberries (craisins)

1 tablespoon cornstarch

½ teaspoon cinnamon

¼ teaspoon nutmeg

Topping:

3 ounces gingersnap cookies (about 12 medium cookies)

¼ cup (packed) brown sugar

¼ cup white sugar

¼ cup all-purpose flour

6 tablespoons cold butter, cut into ½-inch pieces

Heat oven to 375°F. Spray 8-inch-square baking dish with nonstick spray. Add all fruit mixture ingredients, stirring to mix. In food processor, chop gingersnaps very coarsely. Add remaining topping ingredients. Pulse on-and-off a few times until mixture is crumbly, with pieces no larger than the size of a pea. Sprinkle mixture evenly over fruit in baking dish. Bake until the topping is deep golden brown and the fruit is bubbling, 30 to 40 minutes. Cool for at least 45 minutes before serving; best served the day it is made.

Green Gooseberry Jam (no pectin)

1 cup of cleaned gooseberries yields about ¾ cup jam

Green gooseberries contain enough pectin to make jam; once the berries ripen, commercial pectin (which requires precise amounts of fruit, sugar and pectin) needs to be added to make the mixture set up. Since you don't have to mess with pectin in this recipe, it's easy to make a batch of any size. Measurements are given for 1 cup of cleaned gooseberries; adjust proportionally for the amount of gooseberries you've got.

Note: It takes a bit of time to learn how to cook jam without pectin added. It's better to undercook it; you can always cook it a bit more (even after it's cooled) if it's too thin, but if you overcook it, it will be too stiff to use once it's cooled.

6 ounces fresh or previously frozen green gooseberries (about 1 cup)

3 tablespoons water

6 ounces sugar (1 cup minus 2 tablespoons)

Half a thin pat of butter

Place a small ceramic plate in the freezer; this will be used for testing doneness of the jam. Place gooseberries and water in a heavy-bottomed non-aluminum saucepan. Heat over medium heat until simmering, then cover and adjust heat mixture just boils. Cook, covered, for 10 minutes, or until gooseberries are very soft and water has cooked away.

Mash fruit with a potato masher, and place the uncovered saucepan over medium heat. Add a third of the sugar and cook, stirring constantly, for about a minute. Add half of the remaining sugar and cook, stirring constantly, for another minute. Add the remaining sugar and cook for another minute, stirring constantly until all sugar is dissolved.

When sugar has dissolved, add butter; increase heat to high. When the mixture comes to a full boil, cook for 5 minutes, stirring constantly. Remove jam from heat to prevent overcooking while you test for doneness. Place a spoonful on the cold plate and return to the freezer for a minute; finished jam will hold its shape, without weeping around the edges. If the jam is too thin, return to boiling and cook for another minute, then re-test; repeat as needed. Pour into sterilized half-pint canning jars and refrigerate, or process for 10 minutes in a water-bath canner (see pg. 185 for information on sterilizing jars and canning).

Green Gooseberry Filling   About ½ cup; easily increased

This deliciously tart filling is a nice counterpoint when used in sweet or rich recipes.

6 ounces fresh or previously frozen green gooseberries (about 1 cup)

3 tablespoons sugar, or as needed

2 tablespoons grated apple

1 tablespoon orange juice

Chop gooseberries coarsely by hand or in mini food processor. Combine chopped gooseberries, sugar, apple and orange juice in small, heavy-bottomed saucepan. Heat to boiling over medium-high heat, then cook, stirring frequently, until mixture is no longer runny and looks like chunky applesauce; this will take 9 to 11 minutes. Taste for sweetness, and add a little more sugar if you like. Cool before using.

Use this to prepare Easy Bear Claws (pg. 30), Fruit-Striped Cookie Fingers (pg. 145), or Fruit-Filled Muffins (pg. 163). Refrigerate extra filling, and use to top oatmeal or toast.

Gooseberry Pudding Cake

9 servings

Sticky and gooey on the bottom, crispy on top—this is delightful for brunch or dessert.

2½ cups fresh or previously frozen gooseberries (green or ripe; about 1 pound)

Batter:

1⅓ cups all-purpose flour

1 cup sugar

1½ teaspoons baking powder

¼ teaspoon salt

½ cup whole or 2% milk

4 tablespoons (half of a stick) butter, melted and cooled slightly

½ teaspoon vanilla extract

1 egg

Topping:

⅔ cup sugar

2 teaspoons cornstarch

¼ teaspoon cinnamon

⅔ cup boiling water

Heat oven to 350°F. Spray 9-inch-square baking dish with nonstick spray. Scatter gooseberries in dish; set aside.

Prepare the batter: Place wire-mesh strainer over mixing bowl. Add flour, sugar, baking powder and salt; shake strainer to sift into bowl. Add milk, butter and vanilla; beat with electric mixer until smooth. Add egg; beat until well mixed, scraping down sides (batter is thick). Spoon batter evenly over gooseberries, then gently spread to the edges of the pan, covering the gooseberries completely.

Prepare the topping: In small bowl, combine sugar, cornstarch and cinnamon; stir until well mixed. Sprinkle evenly over batter. Gently pour boiling water over the batter. Bake until browned and set, 45 to 50 minutes; a toothpick inserted most of the way down should come out clean (don't stick the toothpick all the way down, because the gooseberry layer is gooey). Cool on wire rack for at least 15 minutes before serving; serve warm or at room temperature.

Strawberry-Gooseberry Dessert Sauce   About 2 cups

Serve this sauce warm or cold. It's good when used to top pound cake, shortcake, ice cream or waffles and can be used in oatmeal for a sweet flavor booster. You may also enjoy it served simply in a dish; try it warm, perhaps with a dollop of whipped cream.

2 cups fresh or previously frozen gooseberries (green or ripe; about 12 ounces)

¾ cup sugar

⅓ cup orange juice or water

1 teaspoon minced fresh gingerroot, optional

A pinch of ground cloves

1 cup sliced strawberries, wild or domestic

1 tablespoon cornstarch, blended with 2 tablespoons water

In saucepan, combine gooseberries, sugar, orange juice, gingerroot and cloves. Heat to boiling; reduce heat and simmer for 10 minutes, stirring occasionally. Add strawberries; cook for about 3 minutes longer. Stir in cornstarch mixture; increase heat to medium-high and cook, stirring constantly, until mixture boils and thickens. Cool slightly before serving or refrigerating.

 This recipe is delicious when prepared with either green or ripe gooseberries. It has a tangier flavor when prepared with green gooseberries.

Other recipes in this book featuring gooseberries:
Six Recipes Using Wild Fruit Juice or Syrup, pgs. 172–176
Wild Berry or Fruit Syrup, pg. 177
Dehydrating Wild Berries and Fruits, pgs. 182–184
Wild Berry or Fruit Leather, pg. 184
As a substitute in Individual Currant Cheesecakes, pg. 55

Quick ideas for using gooseberries:
Substitute gooseberries for cut-up fresh rhubarb in desserts and other recipes.

GRAPES (Riverbank grapes, *Vitis riparia,* and others)

Note: Instructions and recipes on pgs. 70–73 apply to the smaller, thin-skinned wild grapes: riverbank (*Vitis riparia*), summer (*V. aestivalis*), frost (*V. vulpina*), graybark (*V. cinerea*), fox (*V. labrusca*) and catbird (*V. palmata*) grapes. Muscadines (*V. rotundifolia*) are a large, thick-skinned grape found in parts of our area; they are picked and handled differently, and are discussed on pgs. 104–111.

You can store grapes in the refrigerator up to a week; make sure the grapes at the bottom don't get crushed by the grapes above them, or they will start to rot.

Riverbank and the other smaller, thin-skinned grapes discussed here are easy to pick and grow in good quantities, so it's easy to harvest a gallon in a short time. Use scissors to snip off the entire cluster, dropping it into an ice cream pail or large bag. A 1-gallon ice cream pail holds about 3 pounds of grape clusters. When you're ready to process the grapes, rinse them well. I pick the grapes off the stems before processing them; bugs often lurk in the clusters, and by stemming the grapes, I eliminate these pests. (If you've got a large quantity of grapes to process or are using a press, simply remove the largest stems.)

Wild grapes contain tartrate, a substance that causes crystallization in jelly. It burns your skin after prolonged contact, and also burns your mouth if you eat very many raw grapes. Tartrate is removed during juicing. Note that fox grapes (and muscadines) contain far less tartrate than the other wild grapes; they are also the largest of the grapes discussed here, and their skins are thicker.

To prepare juice, place washed grapes in a clean container. Mash with a potato masher, mashing gently to avoid breaking up the bitter seeds. Transfer the mixture to a strainer lined with a triple layer of dampened cheesecloth. Gather the cheesecloth up around the grapes, and squeeze to extract as much juice as possible. Return the fruit-filled cheesecloth to the strainer and open it up; pour about ½ cup water into the fruit pulp, then re-gather the cheesecloth and squeeze again. Return the fruit-filled cheesecloth to the strainer and let it drip for 30 minutes. (Wear clean rubber gloves, or rinse your hands immediately after squeezing the grapes to wash off the tartrate.)

After the crushed grapes have dripped as much as they will, pour the liquid into a clean jar; for each quart of stemmed grapes you started with, you'll have about 1½ cups of juice. Refrigerate for 24 hours; a sediment will develop. Carefully pour off the separated liquid into a clean jar; the sediment is fairly solid, but you should pour slowly to avoid stirring it up, and as soon as it nears the stream of liquid you're pouring, stop. Discard the sediment, which contains the tartrate. The amount of sediment varies; it is typically between one-quarter and one-third the total volume of the freshly pressed juice. So each quart of picked grapes yields 1 to 1¼ cups of finished, deep-purple juice.

Grape Jelly (pectin added)

2½ cups wild grape juice

Half of a 1.75-ounce box powdered pectin

½ teaspoon butter, optional (helps reduce foaming)

3½ cups sugar

Prepare and process as directed in Jelly Instructions (using pectin), pg. 178.

No-Cook Grape Jelly

3 half-pints

Although the pectin mixture is cooked, the juice is never heated, resulting in sparkling-clear jelly with a clean, bright flavor. Jelly making doesn't get much easier than this.

1½ cups wild grape juice

2½ cups sugar

**Half of a 1.75-ounce box powdered pectin
(see pg. 178 for information on dividing pectin)**

⅓ cup plus 1 tablespoon water

Sterilize 3 half-pint jars, bands and new lids as directed on pg. 185. Combine juice and sugar in glass or Pyrex® mixing bowl, stirring to dissolve sugar. Let stand for 10 minutes, stirring occasionally.

In small saucepan, combine pectin and water; stir well (mixture may be lumpy). Heat to a full, rolling boil over high heat, stirring constantly. Cook at a rolling boil for 1 minute, stirring constantly. Pour pectin mixture into juice in bowl. Stir constantly with wooden spoon until sugar is completely dissolved and no longer grainy, about 3 minutes; a few grains may remain, but the mixture should no longer look cloudy (or the jelly will be cloudy).

Pour mixture into prepared jars or containers, leaving ½ inch headspace; cover with clean lids. Let stand at room temperature for 24 hours; the jelly should be set. If it is not set, refrigerate for several days until set before using or freezing; grape jelly may take as long as a week to set. The jelly will keep for 3 weeks in the refrigerator, or it may be frozen for up to a year.

Wild Grape-Black Cherry Wine

8 to 12 bottles

This is a rich, rounded dry red wine with a full mouthfeel and lots of fruit. It uses almost twice as much fresh fruit as other recipes, but the results are worth it.

Winemaking is actually fairly straightforward, but there are a lot of steps and special instructions to follow. The instructions here assume some familiarity with winemaking; if you are unfamiliar with the procedures, consult *First Steps in Winemaking* by C.J.J. Berry, or my book, *Abundantly Wild,* for more information. You can also get help, advice, and supplies such as fermenters and airlocks, from a good winemaking supply store, as well as from some websites.

5 pounds wild grapes or muscadines

5 pounds black cherries or chokecherries, fresh or previously frozen

5 pounds sugar

1½ gallons hot water (not boiling; use hot tap water)

5-gram packet of Montrachet wine yeast

2 Campden tablets, finely crushed

2 teaspoons yeast nutrient

1 teaspoon pectic enzyme

Day 1: Sterilize a 5-gallon container, such as a plastic fermenter or a food-safe 5-gallon plastic bucket, with sulphite solution. Place fruit in sterilized container. Crush fruit with your hands, rinsing hands frequently to wash off tartrate (or wear rubber gloves). Add sugar and hot water; stir well with a sterilized spoon (sterilize by rinsing with sulphite solution or by boiling for 5 minutes). When water cools to 70°F or less, add yeast, Campden tablets, yeast nutrient and pectic enzyme. Cover loosely with muslin. The wine should begin to ferment and bubble in 12 to 24 hours; if it fails to start bubbling, stir with a sterilized spoon to aerate it. When it starts bubbling, the solid ingredients will form a cake on top; this is normal. Let stand for 10 days, stirring occasionally with a sterilized spoon; this stage is called the "primary ferment."

Day 10: Sterilize two clean 1-gallon glass jugs with sulphite solution; also have a half-gallon jug ready in case you need it. Strain liquid through a cheesecloth-lined funnel into the jugs; top off if necessary with white grape juice or water (if you don't have enough for a full second gallon, use the half-gallon jug instead). Cap the jugs with sterilized airlocks and place them in a cool location. The wine will bubble vigorously, and bubbles will come frequently through the airlocks. Ferment for 3 to 4 weeks, until a bubble comes through the airlock only once every minute or two; this stage is called the "secondary ferment."

Day 35 (approximate): The wine will separate into two layers: a top layer of liquid (which may be slightly cloudy) and a bottom layer of sediment. Use a sterilized winemaker's siphon or food-grade plastic hose to siphon the liquid into another sterilized jug, taking care to siphon off only the liquid; avoid disturbing the sediment. This is called "racking." Top off the wine with water as needed to fill the jug to within ½ inch of the top. Re-sterilize the airlock and cap the jug; return it to the cool location. After this, rack the wine as necessary; typically, you'll want to rack it after a month or so because it will have developed another layer of sediment, and again after that as needed. Top off the wine each time with water as needed, and always keep it capped with a sterilized airlock. Fermentation is complete when the water in the airlock is level on both sides; if the water remains pushed up on the release side, fermentation is still occurring, although it may be almost unnoticeable.

Bottling and aging: When you decide that fermentation is complete, use the siphon hose to transfer the wine into clean, sterilized wine bottles. Sterilize new corks, then use a corking device to push the cork into the bottle; if the corker doesn't push the cork all the way in, use the handle of a wooden spoon to complete the job. Many home wine-makers run a piece of sterilized string alongside the cork, push the cork halfway in, then pull out the string. This releases pressure from inside the bottle, allowing you to push the cork all the way in.

Rest the bottles on their sides, and let the wine age for at least a month; longer is better, but don't wait too long before checking it. Most homemade wines are best when drunk within a year of being bottled, although some exceptional homemade wines—like this one, if it is properly made—can be bottle-aged for as much as 10 years.

Other recipes in this book featuring wild grapes:
Six Recipes Using Wild Fruit Juice or Syrup, pgs. 172–176
Wild Berry or Fruit Syrup, pg. 177

Quick ideas for using wild grapes:
Blend the juice with apple juice, using one part grape juice to two parts apple juice (or to taste). Sweeten as needed; chill before serving.

GROUND CHERRIES (*Physalis* spp.)

The *Physalis* family is fairly large, and includes not only ground cherries but tomatillos and the ornamental plant commonly called Chinese lantern. All have a ribbed, papery husk enclosing the fruit, which is a pulpy berry with many soft seeds, rather like a small tomato. You probably won't encounter tomatillos or Chinese lanterns in the wild in our area, just one of the numerous varieties of ground cherry.

In our area, ripe ground cherries range from golden yellow, to orange, to purple; it's important to note that ripe ground cherries are never green or black. If you've picked some ground cherries and they are still greenish, let them ripen on the countertop until they soften and are no longer green. If they remain tinged with green, they shouldn't be eaten; unripe ground cherries are somewhat toxic, as are all other parts of the plant, including the papery husk. The husk should be very loose around the fruit as well. If you have fruits with husks that cling tightly, discard these without tasting; they probably aren't ground cherries.

Ground cherries were a favorite of early settlers, but today the fruit is little known except to foragers and a few country folk who still remember them.

To prepare ground cherries, peel away and discard the papery husk. The berries have a sticky, slightly waxy coating that often holds dust, so they should be rinsed after husking; sometimes, they have dark spots of waxy dirt that can be rubbed off while holding the berry under running water. The seeds in ground cherries are soft and unnoticeable, so they don't need to be removed. A quart of husked ground cherries weighs about 1¼ pounds.

Ground cherries are most commonly cooked into jam or preserves, or used in baked goods such as pies. Most ground cherries can be eaten raw or cooked, although some sources state that smooth ground cherry (*P. longifolia*) should be cooked before eating; I can't verify that in any scientific texts, but wanted to pass it along. Ground cherries keep for several weeks in the refrigerator, and can be frozen for longer-term storage; just pack washed berries into plastic bags or containers and freeze with no further preparation. They also dehydrate well (see pgs. 182–184), and make a nice addition to trail mixes when dried. Ground cherries may cause diarrhea if eaten in large quantities, and persons who are allergic to tomatoes should not eat ground cherries.

Ground Cherry Pie with Cracker Topping

1 pie (6 to 8 servings)

Here's a twist on a top crust. The cracker topping is crunchy and buttery, and works really well with sunny ground cherries.

Topping:

4 ounces buttery crackers such as Ritz

2 tablespoons butter, melted

1 tablespoon sugar

Pastry for single-crust pie

1 Granny Smith or other cooking apple

1½ cups husked, ripe ground cherries (7½ to 8 ounces)

½ cup sugar

2 tablespoons cornstarch

½ teaspoon cinnamon

¼ teaspoon nutmeg

1 tablespoon lemon juice

Heat oven to 375°F. Make the topping: Process crackers in food processor until medium consistency; you may also place them in a plastic bag and bash them with a rolling pin. Place in medium mixing bowl. Drizzle with melted butter; add sugar and mix well. Set aside. Line shallow pie plate (not a deep-dish pie plate) with pastry; flute edges decoratively and set aside.

Peel and core apple, then chop to medium-fine consistency. In large mixing bowl, combine chopped apple, ground cherries, sugar, cornstarch, cinnamon and nutmeg; stir gently to combine. Add lemon juice and stir again. Scrape into prepared crust. Spoon cracker topping evenly over filling. Place pie on a baking sheet (to catch drips); cover pie loosely with foil. Bake for 15 minutes, then remove foil and bake until crumb topping is deep golden brown and filling is bubbly, 20 to 25 minutes longer. Cool on wire rack; best served slightly warm, the day it is made.

 A food processor works best for chopping the apple, and if you used it to crush the crackers, you don't have to rinse it out before chopping the apple.

Ground Cherry Jam (no pectin)

About 3 half-pints

1 quart husked, ripe ground cherries (about 1¼ pounds)

2 cups sugar

¼ cup water

¼ cup freshly squeezed lemon juice

1 cinnamon stick, optional

Please read the notes on no-pectin jam in the Green Gooseberry Jam recipe (pg. 66). Ground cherries have less pectin than green gooseberries, so they require longer cooking, but the basic technique is the same.

In heavy-bottomed non-aluminum 2-quart pot, combine all ingredients. Heat to boiling over high heat, then reduce heat to medium and mash slightly with a potato masher (don't break up the cinnamon stick). Cook fruit at a moderate boil for 30 minutes. Remove jam from the heat to prevent overcooking while you test for doneness. Place a spoonful on a cool plate and place in the freezer for a few minutes; the jam should hold its shape, without weeping around the edges. If the jam is too thin, return to boiling and cook for another few minutes, then re-test; continue as needed until the consistency is correct. Discard cinnamon stick. Pour into sterilized half-pint canning jars; refrigerate for storage, or process for 10 minutes in a water-bath canner (see pg. 185).

Ground Cherry Filling

About ½ cup; easily increased

¾ teaspoon water

¾ teaspoon cornstarch

5½ ounces husked, ripe ground cherries (about 1 heaping cup)

1 tablespoon sugar

¼ teaspoon vanilla extract

In small bowl, blend together water and cornstarch; set aside. Chop ground cherries coarsely by hand or in mini food processor. In small, heavy-bottomed saucepan, combine ground cherries, sugar and vanilla. Heat to boiling over medium-high heat, then cook, stirring frequently, until mixture is no longer runny; this will take 8 to 10 minutes. Add cornstarch mixture, stirring constantly; cook for 1 to 2 minutes longer, or until thick. Cool before using.

Use this to prepare Easy Bear Claws (pg. 30), Fruit-Striped Cookie Fingers (pg. 145), or Fruit-Filled Muffins (pg. 163). Refrigerate extra filling, and use to top oatmeal or toast.

Ground Cherry Custard Bars

½ cup (1 stick) butter, softened

1 cup all-purpose flour

¼ cup powdered sugar

1 cup husked, ripe ground cherries (about 5 ounces)

Custard:

½ cup sugar

3 tablespoons all-purpose flour

¼ teaspoon salt

½ cup whole milk

2 tablespoons freshly squeezed lemon juice

1 teaspoon vanilla extract

3 egg yolks

Heat oven to 350°F. In a large bowl, beat butter with electric mixer until light. Add flour and powdered sugar; beat at low speed until well combined (mixture will be crumbly). Press mixture firmly into the bottom and ½ inch up the sides of an 8-inch-square baking dish. Bake 15 minutes. While crust is baking, prepare the filling; if the 15 minutes is up before the filling is ready, remove the crust from the oven and set it aside.

To start on the filling: With a very sharp knife, cut the ground cherries into quarters and set aside. Make the custard: Stir sugar, flour and salt together in a heavy-bottomed non-aluminum saucepan. In measuring cup, combine milk, lemon juice, vanilla and egg yolks; stir with a fork to break up and beat in the egg yolks. Slowly add milk mixture to sugar mixture in saucepan, whisking constantly; whisk until smooth. Cook over medium heat, stirring almost constantly, until mixture thickens, about 5 minutes. Remove from heat; stir in ground cherries.

Scrape custard mixture into baked crust, spreading evenly. Return to oven and bake until custard is set, 30 to 35 minutes. Cool completely; cut into 16 squares.

Chicken Salad with Ground Cherries and Almonds

4 servings

A lovely luncheon dish. Serve with warm biscuits and chilled iced tea.

1 pound cooked chicken breast, diced

2 green onions, chopped

½ cup finely diced celery

¼ cup mayonnaise (reduced-fat works fine)

1 tablespoon chopped fresh tarragon

1 cup husked, ripe ground cherries (about 5 ounces)*

¼ cup olive oil

1 tablespoon white wine vinegar

2 teaspoons orange juice

½ teaspoon Dijon mustard

Salt and pepper

4 to 5 cups tender salad greens

½ cup sliced almonds

In mixing bowl, stir together chicken, onions, celery, mayonnaise and tarragon; set aside (or refrigerate, if preparing in advance).

When you're ready to serve, cut ground cherries into halves; set aside. Prepare salad dressing: In a small jar, combine oil, vinegar, orange juice and mustard; cover and shake vigorously. Add salt and pepper to taste. In a large bowl, toss dressing with greens. Divide greens between 4 salad plates. Top each with one-quarter of the chicken salad, mounding attractively. Scatter ground cherries over the salad; top with almonds. Serve immediately.

*Some sources say that smooth ground cherry (*Physalis longifolia*) should not be eaten raw, so it is best to prepare this with a different species.

You can prepare the chicken salad mixture in advance and keep in the refrigerator until you're ready to serve; dress the greens and assemble the salad right before serving so the greens stay crisp.

Sweet and Snappy Ground Cherry Salsa About 1 cup

The fruity, sweet taste of ground cherries makes a wonderful foil to the bite of hot peppers and the tang of fresh cilantro. Enjoy this salsa with chicken fajitas, bean burritos or tostadas, or warm tortilla chips.

1 clove garlic

1 or 2 fresh jalapeño peppers, depending on heat level desired

About ¼ cup fresh cilantro leaves

1 cup husked, ripe ground cherries* (about 5 ounces)

One-quarter of a medium red onion

1 tablespoon seasoned rice vinegar

¼ teaspoon salt, or to taste

Place garlic in food processor and chop until fine. Add pepper(s) and pulse on and off a few times. Add cilantro and process until everything is finely chopped. Transfer mixture to small mixing bowl. Add ground cherries to food processor and chop to medium consistency; the texture doesn't have to be completely even so don't worry if there are a few larger chunks of fruit in the mix. Transfer ground cherries to mixing bowl. Cut onion into ¼-inch dice; add to mixing bowl. Add vinegar and salt. Stir well to mix. Let stand for 15 minutes, then taste for seasoning and adjust salt if necessary. Serve at room temperature; refrigerate leftovers.

*Some sources say that smooth ground cherry (*Physalis longifolia*) should not be eaten raw, so it is best to prepare this with a different species.

 This is a very juicy salsa, so you may want to place a fork rather than a spoon into the serving dish. Use any leftover liquid to add spice to a pot of beans or a stir-fry.

Other recipes in this book featuring ground cherries:
Dehydrated Wild Berries and Fruits, pgs. 182–184
Wild Berry or Fruit Leather, pg. 184

Quick ideas for using ground cherries:
Cut in half and add to fruit salads or green salads (note the comment in the intro text on pg. 74 regarding raw ground cherries).
Add dehydrated ground cherries to oatmeal or other hot cereal, either during or after cooking.

HACKBERRIES and SUGARBERRIES
(Celtis occidentalis, C. laevigata)

Hackberry is common in urban areas, yet few people notice its fruit; fewer still realize that the small, dark, berry-like drupe is edible and tasty. A few texts refer to the tree as "sugarberry," and mention that the sweet fruit is used primarily as a trail nibble; several note that Native Americans used dried, crushed sugarberry to season venison. Sugarberry is actually a related, similar tree that is found along rural roads and in forests in the southern half of our area.

Hackberries and sugarberries have a large pit, with thin flesh. But the pit is edible, especially with proper preparation, and the fruit is sweet.

The flesh of both species is dry but very sweet, with a flavor reminiscent of dates, apples and oranges mixed together. Unfortunately, there is precious little of it; most of the fruit consists of a large pit. Unlike the hard stones in cherries and plums, however, hackberry and sugarberry pits are edible; they are brittle but soft enough to chew. The sensation is unusual, and trail nibblers usually discard the pit.

Pillow Cookies with Hackberry or Sugarberry Filling

About 30 cookies

The sweet filling has an unusual texture from the pits. This is a recipe I developed for my book, Abundantly Wild: Collecting and Cooking Wild Edibles in the Upper Midwest.

Filling:

⅔ cup hackberry or sugarberry fruits, stems removed

⅓ cup sugar

½ cup water

½ cup chopped pecans or other nuts

Dough:

½ cup (1 stick) unsalted butter, softened

½ cup (packed) brown sugar

½ cup white sugar

1 egg

1 teaspoon lemon extract, orange extract or vanilla extract

½ teaspoon baking soda

½ teaspoon salt

2 cups all-purpose flour

See companion *Wild Berries & Fruits Field Guide of IN, KY and OH*– page 302

First, prepare the filling. Pound fruits with mortar and pestle until pits are well pulverized; for the least crunchy filling, pound until fruits are reduced to a smooth paste. (Tip: It's easiest to work in small batches of a tablespoon or two at a time; this way, no large chunks of pit will escape your notice. Scrape pounded fruit into a small saucepan as you go, and continue until all fruit has been pounded.)

Combine pounded fruit with sugar and water in small saucepan. Heat over medium heat, stirring constantly, until boiling gently. Cook for 4 minutes or until thick, stirring constantly. Stir in pecans. Remove from heat and let cool completely before assembling the cookies.

To make dough, cream butter in mixing bowl with electric mixer. Gradually add brown and white sugars, beating until smooth. Add egg, extract, baking soda and salt; beat well. Add flour and beat just until mixed. If you prepare the dough right after cooking the filling, gather the dough into a ball, wrap it tightly and refrigerate until you're ready to bake. Or, simply prepare dough after the filling has cooled, and proceed immediately to baking.

When you're ready to bake, heat oven to 350°F. Lightly spray 2 baking sheets with non-stick spray; set aside. Roll out half of the dough about ⅛ inch thick, or just a bit thicker. Cut into 2-inch circles with a glass or cookie cutter. Place half of the circles on prepared baking sheet, allowing ½ inch between circles. Place 1 teaspoon filling mixture in center of each circle, keeping it away from edges. Place a circle of dough over each mound of filling, forming it into a gentle dome shape over filling and gently pressing the edges together (they will seal together during baking, so don't worry about pressing too hard). Repeat with remaining ingredients to fill the second baking sheet. Bake until golden brown, 13 to 15 minutes. Cool before serving.

Hackberry and sugarberry pits are very crunchy even when crushed fairly fine. It is an odd sensation to encounter in a cookie—not unpleasant, just unexpected, rather like finding a piece of eggshell that accidentally got into the dough. But unlike the eggshell, the pieces of pit can be chewed and swallowed. The more time you spend pounding the fruit with the mortar and pestle, the smoother and less crunchy the filling will be.

HAWTHORNS *(Crataegus* spp.)

Numerous varieties of hawthorn grow in our area, and it's hard to know exactly which species you've found. The fruit, usually called a haw, looks like a crabapple, but the seeds in the fruit are larger. Haws of some varieties, or from individual trees, are small, and there is very little flesh in proportion to the seeds. Nevertheless, what flesh and skin there is has a lot of flavor, so these small haws can be used to make juice. If you're lucky, however, you'll find a tree whose fruits are large, soft and fleshy. These haws have enough flesh to make jam; or, the seeds can be removed and the fruit used in pies and other baked goods. The flavor of a good haw is outstanding—rather like a pear with apple and almond overtones.

All hawthorn fruits are edible. The best for cooking have a large amount of fruit in proportion to the seeds; these can be cut up and used like crabapples.

To prepare large haws for use in pies or other recipes that use pieces of fruit rather than pulp, I use a table knife to cut or break them open. My feeling is that if I have to use a sharp knife, either the haw isn't ripe enough, or it is too hard because it's nothing but seeds. Once the haw is open, scrape out the seeds and any blackish tissue surrounding them; if soft, clean flesh adheres to the seeds, scrape it off with the knife before discarding the seed. Pull or cut away the blossom end and the stem, then feel the flesh carefully with your fingertips to be sure there isn't a tooth-shattering seed hidden in the piece. Place the cleaned, seedless haw chunks, and any flesh you've scraped from the seeds, into a measuring cup. Because haws vary so much in size, it's hard to predict the yield; in general, you'll get about ½ cup of cleaned, ready-to-cook haw chunks from a pound of whole, large haws (roughly a quart, give or take).

To prepare hawthorn juice, place whole haws in non-aluminum pot. Add water to generously cover the fruit. Heat to boiling over high heat, then reduce heat and boil gently for 20 minutes, or until the fruit is very soft. Mash as best you can with a potato masher, making sure that each fruit has been opened. Add a little more water if it looks too dry, and cook for 5 minutes longer; the pulpy, seedy mixture should be well covered with water. Transfer the mixture to a strainer lined with doubled, dampened cheesecloth and let it drip for 30 minutes; if you're making jelly, don't squeeze the fruit or the jelly will be cloudy. After the clear liquid has dripped away, set it aside and squeeze the fruit into a different container; you can use this slightly cloudy juice as a beverage or for cooking. Yield varies quite a bit, because hawthorns vary in size; in general, you'll get 1½ cups of pink juice per pound of hawthorns.

Hawthorn and Sausage Brunch Casserole
6 to 8 servings

Hawthorns work really well with the sausage and cheese in this simple dish. It's a natural for brunch, or even a light supper.

8 ounces breakfast-style pork sausage (casings removed if links)

¼ cup diced onion

1¼ cups whole or 2% milk

3 eggs

½ teaspoon dry mustard powder

4 or 5 slices day-old firm white bread (Italian bread works well)

¾ to 1 cup cleaned, seedless hawthorn chunks

1½ cups shredded mozzarella cheese, divided

Heat oven to 375°F. Spray an 8-inch-square baking dish with nonstick spray; set aside. In medium skillet, cook sausage over medium heat, stirring to break up, until no longer pink. Drain off excess grease. Add onion and cook, stirring frequently, until sausage is lightly browned and onion is tender, about 5 minutes. Set aside to cool slightly.

In large mixing bowl, combine milk, eggs and mustard powder; beat well with a fork and set aside. Now, use a blender to make fresh breadcrumbs. Start by tearing bread into 1-inch chunks. Turn the blender on high. Drop chunks from one slice into the blender, immediately re-covering it; the bread pops up very high and can make quite a mess if you don't keep it covered. Process until bread has been chopped into medium-fine crumbs. Transfer breadcrumbs to a large bowl; repeat with remaining bread. Measure 2½ cups of crumbs; if you have extra crumbs, see tip below.

Add measured crumbs, sausage mixture, hawthorn chunks and 1 cup of the cheese to the milk mixture. Stir well, then scrape into prepared dish. Bake, uncovered, for 25 minutes. Sprinkle remaining cheese over the casserole; bake for 5 minutes longer, or until cheese has melted. Remove from oven and let stand 10 minutes before serving.

Substitution: Use crabapple chunks, cored and cut up, in place of the hawthorns; you could also substitute cut-up wild pears.

If you have any breadcrumbs remaining, you can spread them out on a baking sheet and let them dry at room temperature for a few days, stirring occasionally; when completely dry, store in a jar and use in any recipe calling for dry breadcrumbs.

Hawthorn Jelly

3 cups hawthorn juice

Half of a 1.75-ounce box powdered pectin

½ teaspoon butter, optional (helps reduce foaming)

3 cups sugar

Prepare and process as directed in Jelly Instructions (using pectin), pg. 178.

Variation: Use a mix of hawthorn and crabapple juice for a lovely, pinkish Hawthorn-Crabapple Jelly.

Other recipes in this book featuring hawthorns:
Fruits of the Forest Pie, pg. 170
Six Recipes Using Wild Fruit Juice or Syrup, pgs. 172–176
Wild Berry or Fruit Syrup, pg. 177

Quick ideas for using hawthorns:
Use the juice in place of apple juice, for cooking or as a beverage.
Use hawthorn chunks to substitute for chopped apple or pear in recipes for baked goods. Watch out for the seeds when eating!

HIGHBUSH CRANBERRIES *(Viburnum trilobum)*

Although unrelated to true cranberries (*Vaccinium macrocarpon* and others), highbush cranberry fruits taste remarkably like their namesake. They contain a single flat seed, which is hard and bitter, so they must be processed differently than true cranberries. They also have a foul-tasting look-alike, the guelder rose or European cranberry (*Viburnum opulus*). At a quick glance, it's tough to distinguish between these two plants. The easiest way is to simply taste a ripe fruit. If it tastes like a cranberry with just a slight tang of bitterness, harvest away; if it's a guelder rose, you probably won't want to pick any because the fruit is extremely bitter. It's not toxic—although large quantities may cause intestinal problems—so it's safe to sample one.

I've noticed that fruits on highbush cranberry plants often look sparse because they are quickly picked over by birds, while guelder rose plants at the same time are copious with fruit—possibly ignored until the birds have no choice.

Highbush cranberries grow in large clusters on the plants, so it's easy to harvest a good quantity. They can be picked when bright red but still hard, or later, when the fruits have softened naturally. If you pick more than you can process, simply pull the fruits off the clusters and freeze them; when thawed, they will be soft and can be processed without cooking. A 1-gallon ice cream pail full of clusters will yield about 2 quarts of cleaned fruits (after the stems have been removed), weighing about 2½ pounds.

Highbush cranberries must be juiced or puréed before using in recipes. Fruits picked when soft, or softened in the freezer, can be processed without cooking; fruits picked when still hard must be stewed first. To stew highbush cranberries, pull off the stems, measure the fruits and place in a non-aluminum pot. For purée, add 1 cup water per quart of stemless fruit; for juice, add 3 cups water per quart of fruit. Heat to boiling, then reduce the heat; cover and simmer for about 5 minutes, gently crushing with a potato masher near the end. If you're working with uncooked fruits which were soft when picked, or have been softened in the freezer, simply combine the fruits with the appropriate amount of water in a clean bucket, and gently crush with a potato masher.

For juice, transfer the prepared fruit to a strainer lined with doubled, dampened cheesecloth and let it drip for 30 minutes; if you're making jelly, don't squeeze the fruit or the jelly will be cloudy. After the clear liquid has dripped away, set it aside and squeeze the fruit into a different container; you can use this slightly cloudy juice as a beverage or for cooking. **For purée,** process the prepared fruit through a food mill, discarding the seeds. A quart of stemmed fruits will yield about 3¼ cups of juice, or about 2 cups of purée.

Highbush cranberries are rich in vitamin C; the purée or juice can be added to other fruits when baking, or sweetened and used on its own. The juice is often used to make delicious jelly; the purée can be used to make jam. In his book, *The Forager's Harvest*, wild foods specialist Sam Thayer writes that juice or purée made from fruits that were picked when soft (or softened in the freezer) and processed without stewing taste better than those made from fruits which have been stewed.

Highbush Cranberry Spice Cake

This cake gets its delightful flavor from the highbush cranberries and the spices. The cream cheese frosting is the perfect finish, but a sprinkling of powdered sugar also works well.

6 tablespoons unsalted butter, softened

⅔ cup white sugar

½ cup (packed) golden brown sugar

1 egg

1¼ cups all-purpose flour

¾ teaspoon cinnamon

¾ teaspoon baking powder

½ teaspoon baking soda

¼ teaspoon ground cloves

⅛ teaspoon nutmeg

⅔ cup highbush cranberry purée

½ cup golden raisins

½ cup chopped walnuts

Cream Cheese Frosting (pg. 87) or powdered sugar

Heat oven to 350°F. Spray 8-inch-square baking dish with nonstick spray; set aside. In large mixing bowl, beat butter with electric mixer until light. Add white and brown sugars; beat for about 1 minute. Add egg; beat about 1 minute longer.

Place a wire-mesh strainer on a dinner plate. Add flour, cinnamon, baking powder, baking soda, cloves and nutmeg. Shake strainer over the mixing bowl to sift about half of the flour into the butter mixture. Add half of the highbush cranberry purée to the butter mixture; stir well with wooden spoon. Sift remaining flour into mixture; add remaining purée and stir until combined. Stir in raisins and nuts. Scrape into prepared pan, spreading evenly. Bake until a toothpick inserted in the center comes out clean, 35 to 40 minutes. Transfer pan to wire rack and let stand until cool. Frost with Cream Cheese Frosting, or sprinkle with powdered sugar if you prefer.

Cream Cheese Frosting
About 1 cup

4 tablespoons (half of a stick) butter, softened

4 ounces cream cheese, softened (reduced-fat works fine)

1 teaspoon vanilla extract

1 cup powdered sugar

In large mixing bowl, beat butter, cream cheese and vanilla with electric mixer on high until light and fluffy. Hold a wire-mesh strainer over the bowl and add powdered sugar to strainer. Shake strainer to sift into the butter. Beat until smooth. Refrigerate leftover cake for storage if using cream cheese frosting.

Highbush Cranberry Jam
About ¾ cup jam per cup of purée

Make as much of this as you wish; since no pectin is needed, you aren't restricted to specific measurements. For a slightly different flavor, use red wine or port instead of water when stewing the berries (or when mashing berries that you are processing without cooking).

1 cup highbush cranberry purée

½ cup sugar

**1 teaspoon finely grated orange zest
(colored rind only, with none of the white pith)**

¼ teaspoon ground allspice

¼ teaspoon cinnamon

Pinch of ground nutmeg

Combine all ingredients in heavy-bottomed small saucepan. Heat to boiling, then reduce heat and cook at a very gentle boil, stirring frequently, until mixture is thickened to jam-like consistency. Cooking time is typically 45 minutes to an hour, depending on how loose the purée is. Transfer to sterilized jar(s). Store in refrigerator, or freeze for longer storage.

 Some people use guelder rose fruits for jelly and jam, following recipes for highbush cranberries. The fruits smell truly awful when cooking, and a bit of that lingers in the finished product; guelder rose also needs more sugar to make it edible. Don't eat too much of any guelder rose product until you're sure it won't upset your stomach.

Highbush Cranberry Jelly

5 half-pints

3 cups highbush cranberry juice

Half of a 1.75-ounce box powdered pectin

½ teaspoon butter, optional (helps reduce foaming)

3½ cups sugar

Prepare and process as directed in Jelly Instructions (using pectin), pg. 178.

Highbush Sunrise

Per serving

Bright red highbush cranberry syrup stands in for the grenadine in the classic tequila sunrise —a delightful difference!

2 ounces gold tequila

4 to 6 ounces top-quality orange juice

1 tablespoon highbush cranberry syrup (pg. 177)

Orange slice and maraschino cherry, for garnish

Fill a tall glass with ice. Add tequila first, then the orange juice. Now pour the syrup into the glass, as close to the side as possible; it should settle to the bottom and then slowly rise to the top. Garnish with orange slice and cherry. (If your syrup isn't thick enough, the sunrise effect may not work—just stir and enjoy.)

Other recipes in this book featuring highbush cranberries:
>Wild Berry Vinegar, pg. 19
>Six Recipes Using Wild Fruit Juice or Syrup, pgs. 172–176
>Wild Berry or Fruit Syrup, pg. 177
>As a substitute in Autumn Olive "Berries" for Baking, pg. 14
>As a variation in Elderberry Meringue Pie, pg. 60

Quick ideas for using highbush cranberries:
>Stir a few tablespoons of the purée into apple, berry or other fruit pie fillings.
>Mix 1 part highbush cranberry juice with 2 or 3 parts apple juice;
>>sweeten to taste.

JUNIPER, COMMON *(Juniperus communis)*

Juniper is a spice plant, with berry-like fruits that are used as seasoning. They have a sharp, clean scent and taste; they are one of the main ingredients used in the traditional distillation of gin, and they have the same smell. They're usually used in marinades or rubs for meat, and are particularly good with strongly flavored meats such as venison and lamb. Some old-world sausages also use juniper as one of the seasoning ingredients.

Pick juniper fruits in late summer or fall, when they are fully developed and blue, with a dusty bloom. Dry them for a few days at room temperature, then store in a tightly sealed spice bottle in a dark cupboard; they'll keep until the next season.

Red Cabbage with Juniper and Bacon   4 servings

This is a hearty dish that goes well with roasted meats or poultry.

¼ pound thick-cut bacon, cut into ½-inch pieces

Half of a small head of red cabbage, cored and cut into 1-inch chunks

Half of a white onion, cut vertically into ¼-inch-wide wedges

¼ cup chicken broth

3 or 4 juniper fruits, crushed

1 tablespoon white wine vinegar

½ teaspoon dried thyme

In large skillet, sauté bacon over medium heat until crisp. Use slotted spoon to transfer to a plate lined with paper towels; discard all but 1 tablespoon of the drippings. Add cabbage and onion to skillet with drippings. Cook over medium heat, stirring occasionally, for about 5 minutes. Add chicken broth, juniper fruits, vinegar and thyme. Cover and cook for 10 minutes, stirring occasionally. Uncover and cook until juices thicken and cabbage is tender, about 5 minutes longer. Sprinkle bacon over cabbage, stirring to combine; cook for a minute or two, until bacon is hot. Serve immediately.

Other recipes in this book featuring juniper fruits:
Venison Roast with Mountain Ash and Juniper Rub, pg. 97

Quick ideas for using juniper fruits:
Use in any recipe calling for purchased juniper berries.
Simmer crushed juniper fruits in melted butter, then use the mixture to baste poultry while it is roasting.

MAYPOPS (Passiflora incarnata)

Maypops are the fruit of the purple passionflower vine. This stunning flower grows as a roadside weed; it is a vigorous plant, and often covers fences, posts, buildings and mailboxes. While some may consider it a nuisance due to its spreading habit, foragers are always happy to see it, for the fruits are a delicious treat; it has a sweet-tart taste with tropical overtones. Herbalists prepare a sedative from maypops, and eating the fruits may make some people drowsy.

Wherever passionflowers grow, kids seem to delight in jumping on the fruit to make it "pop." A far better use is to enjoy the fruit fresh, or to juice it and use in the recipes in this section.

Maypops look like leathery-skinned greenish hen's eggs, and can be found hanging from the passionflower vines throughout late summer; due to the plant's abundance, it's usually easy to gather a large quantity of maypops in a short time.

The outer skin has a thick, spongy layer of white underneath it; inside, there are dozens of small, brittle seeds, each encased in gel-like pulp. Ripe maypops may be green or yellowish, and the shells may be smooth or wrinkled slightly. It's best to judge ripeness by the relative weight of the fruit, a trick I learned from foraging expert Sam Thayer. Heavier fruits are filled with ripe pulp; lighter fruits will be underripe, or may even be mostly hollow. If you've gathered slightly underripe maypops, let them ripen at room temperature for a few days; the flavor won't be quite as good as vine-ripened maypops. Ripe maypops are excellent simply eaten out of the shell, or scooped into a dish and topped with a little lightly sweetened cream. The seeds are brittle and crunchy, but can be eaten.

Cut the fruit in half crosswise and use a teaspoon to scoop the pulpy seed mass out of the spongy shell. When maypops are ripe, the seed mass comes out easily and cleanly; you will get about a heaping tablespoon of seedy pulp from each average-sized fruit. If you're eating the pulpy seeds whole, pull away and discard the three spongy white ribs attached to the seed mass; if you're preparing maypop juice in the traditional manner, the ribs don't need to be removed. A pound of maypops (15 to 20 average-sized fruits) will yield about 2 cups of seedy pulp.

To prepare maypop juice in the traditional manner, measure the seedy pulp and transfer to a saucepan; add 1 cup of water for each 2 cups of pulp. Heat to boiling over medium-high heat, then cover, reduce heat and simmer for 15 minutes, stirring occasionally. Transfer the mixture to a strainer lined with doubled, dampened cheesecloth and let it drip for 30 minutes; if you're making jelly, don't squeeze the fruit or the jelly will be cloudy. After the clear liquid has dripped away, set it aside and squeeze the fruit into a different container; you can use this slightly cloudy juice as a beverage or for cooking. Two cups of seedy pulp, prepared in this way, will yield about 1¼ cups of clear juice, or 1½ cups of slightly thicker, less-clear juice if you squeeze the entire batch of cooked fruit.

As an option to the traditional, cooked method, I also discovered an easy way to prepare fresh, uncooked maypop juice; please see "Maypops and the Blender" on pg. 94. The juice from this method is slightly cloudy, but it has a fresher taste than cooked juice.

Maypop Milk Punch

This is delightfully refreshing and different: a frothy, milky punch served over crushed ice. Milk punch traditionally has brandy or bourbon in it; this version is delicious without any alcohol, but you can add some as noted, if you like.

- **¾ cup cold milk (2% or whole)**
- **3 tablespoons seedy maypop pulp**
- **1 tablespoon honey**
- **A good pinch of nutmeg**
- **2 tablespoons brandy, optional**

Combine all ingredients in a blender. Blend on high speed for 10 seconds. Let stand for about 30 seconds, then pour into a glass filled with crushed ice; if you like, stop pouring before the last tablespoon or so comes out, since the seeds will have settled to the bottom. You could also pour the full amount into the glass; the seeds will settle to the bottom and can be left unconsumed when the drink is finished, or they can be chewed while enjoying the drink.

Maypop-Orange Drink

This healthful, easy drink has a subtle tropical taste. It's delicious for breakfast, or as an unusual pre-dinner sipper.

- **1 large navel orange, peeled and sectioned, seeds removed**
- **¾ cup cold water, divided**
- **1 teaspoon honey, or to taste**
- **3 to 4 tablespoons seedy maypop pulp**

In blender, combine orange segments, ½ cup of the water, and the honey. Blend on high speed for 10 seconds. Add the maypop pulp; blend for 10 seconds longer. Pour into a wire-mesh strainer that is set over a bowl; let drip for a few minutes, then pour remaining ¼ cup water over the mixture, stirring to let the water mix with the pulpy leftovers in the strainer. Drain for another minute or so, stirring with a spoon. Discard pulp from strainer. Serve drink immediately, or chill until served.

Crispy Halibut with Maypop Sauce

This sauce has an intriguing flavor, and pairs very well with the crispy fish.

1½ cups chicken broth

½ to ¾ cup seedy maypop pulp

2 portion-sized pieces (5 to 6 ounces each; must be at least ¾ inch thick) of skinless halibut or other firm white fish

Salt and pepper

⅓ cup all-purpose flour

1 egg, lightly beaten

⅓ cup fine, dry breadcrumbs

2 tablespoons extra virgin olive oil

3 tablespoons diced onion

⅓ cup cream sherry or apple juice

1 tablespoon unsalted butter

1 tablespoon snipped fresh chives

Combine broth and maypop pulp in a small, heavy-bottomed saucepan. Heat just to boiling; reduce heat so mixture bubbles gently and cook for 15 minutes. While mixture is cooking, heat oven to 375°F. Place a wire-mesh strainer over a medium bowl; set aside until needed. When maypop mixture has cooked for 15 minutes, remove from heat and set aside.

Rinse fish in cold water; pat dry with paper towels. Season to taste with salt and pepper. Dredge in flour, shaking off the excess; reserve remaining flour. Dip floured fish into beaten egg, turning to coat. Dredge in breadcrumbs.

In medium skillet, heat oil over medium-high heat until it shimmers. Add fish, placing the most attractive side down. Cook until nicely browned, about 4 minutes. Flip carefully, and brown the second side. Remove from heat; transfer fish to an oven-safe dish and place in hot oven. You will be preparing the sauce while the fish is baking, and it's easy to lose track of time. To prevent overcooking the fish, set a timer for the expected cooking time (see "Calculating Cooking Time for Fish," pg. 93); when the fish is just cooked, remove it from the oven and cover loosely with foil.

As soon as the fish is in the oven, begin preparing the sauce. Pour off all but a thin film of oil from the skillet, and return it to medium heat. Add onion and cook, stirring occasionally, for about a minute. Pour the sherry into the skillet, watching out for steam. When the sherry has cooked down to a few tablespoons, add the maypop mixture. Increase heat to high and cook for 5 minutes; the liquid should be reduced to about 1 cup in volume. Pour the mixture into the wire-mesh strainer and set it aside to drip. Wipe out the small saucepan with a paper towel.

Melt the butter over medium heat in the cleaned saucepan. Whisk in 1 tablespoon of the leftover flour; continue whisking until smooth. Cook, whisking frequently, until the mixture is bubbly and thickened, about 3 minutes. Use a spoon to press on the maypop mixture in the wire-mesh strainer, extracting as much liquid as possible. Whisking constantly, add the strained liquid to the saucepan with the butter-flour mixture (discard solids from strainer). Cook until smooth and sauce-like, 3 to 5 minutes, then stir in chives. Transfer fish to individual serving plates. Pour a little sauce over each piece. Serve immediately, passing remaining sauce on the side.

Calculating Cooking Time for Fish

If you're preparing fish by broiling, frying, grilling or baking in a hot (450°F) oven, it's easy to figure out how long to cook it: simply measure the thickness at the thickest part. Using any of the methods listed here, fish will be done in 10 minutes per inch of thickness. If your fish is ¾ inch at the thickest point, it will need about 7 minutes of cooking time, and if it is 1¼ inches at the thickest point, it will be done in 12 to 13 minutes. When properly cooked, the flesh should be just opaque when probed with a knife at the thickest point.

The recipe featured on this spread, Crispy Halibut with Maypop Sauce, uses the same basic principles, but because the fish has been pre-browned, it is baked at a lower oven temperature.

Maypop Jelly

4 half-pints

2¾ cups clear maypop juice

Two-thirds of a 1.75-ounce box powdered pectin

¼ teaspoon butter, optional (helps reduce foaming)

3 cups sugar

Prepare and process as directed in Jelly Instructions (using pectin), pg. 178.

Sleepy Time Maypop Toddy

Many people enjoy a hot milk toddy when sleeplessness strikes. The addition of maypop makes this classic even more relaxing—and delicious.

2 to 3 tablespoons seedy maypop pulp

1 cup milk

1 to 2 teaspoons honey, or to taste

A pinch each of cinnamon and nutmeg

Combine maypops and milk in a blender. Blend on high speed for 10 seconds. Strain through fine wire-mesh strainer into a small saucepan. Add honey. Heat over medium heat until a ring of tiny bubbles forms around the edge, stirring to dissolve the honey. Pour into a mug; sprinkle with cinnamon and nutmeg. (If you prefer, strain the mixture from the blender into a mug, and warm in the microwave instead of on the stovetop. Be careful that the milk does not foam up and boil over; stir well before drinking.)

Variation: Substitute maple syrup, white sugar, brown sugar, stevia or your sweetener of choice for the honey.

Maypops and the Blender

The biggest problem with using maypops in recipes is the hard, black seeds. Every wild-foods book I've seen instructs to boil the seedy maypop pulp with water, then strain it through a jelly bag, to obtain maypop juice. But I discovered that the blender does a fine job of making fresh, uncooked maypop juice, and it takes only a few minutes. Here's my technique.

Remove and discard the three white ribs that are attached to the seedy maypop pulp. Combine equal parts of the pulp and water in a blender. Process on HIGH for 10 seconds, then pour into a fine-screen wire-mesh strainer that's set over a bowl. Let it drip for a few minutes, then stir with a spoon to get the last of the liquid out. Discard the black seeds from the strainer. You'll end up with slightly thick maypop liquid, which will separate into two layers as it sits. In my experiments, 1 cup of seedy pulp (from 7 to 10 average maypops) combined with 1 cup water will yield about 1½ cups of maypop liquid.

Maypop Ice Cream

This light and creamy dessert is made without the use of an ice cream freezer.

> **1 extra-large egg (purchase pasteurized eggs if concerned about salmonella)**
>
> **1 cup maypop liquid (processed in a blender and strained; see pg. 94)**
>
> **½ cup sugar**
>
> **½ teaspoon vanilla extract**
>
> **¾ cup heavy cream**
>
> **Ice cubes and cold water for ice-water bath**

Separate the egg, placing the white into a large mixing bowl; place in refrigerator until needed. Add the yolk to a small, heavy-bottomed saucepan; whisk in the maypop liquid, sugar and vanilla. Cook over medium heat, whisking constantly, until mixture begins to simmer. Simmer for 5 minutes, whisking constantly, then remove from heat. Fill a metal baking dish about halfway with cold water; place the saucepan in it, and add ice cubes to the water around the outside of the pan. Let stand, whisking frequently, until the mixture is cool, about 10 minutes.

With a hand mixer on the highest speed, beat the egg white until stiff peaks form, 2 to 4 minutes. Pour maypop mixture into egg whites, and whisk gently to blend. Cover the mixing bowl with foil or plastic wrap, and place into the freezer. Stir every 45 minutes with a wooden spoon until the consistency is like slightly soft ice cream, about 3 hours (four stirrings). Let it freeze for another 45 minutes before serving. For longer storage, scrape it into a freezer-safe container and seal tightly; it will keep for a week or more. If it is too hard to scoop, place container in the refrigerator for 20 minutes before serving.

Quick ideas for using maypops:

Add maypop juice to smoothies or any other fruit-based beverage.

MOUNTAIN ASH *(Sorbus* spp.)

Most people who see these lovely, highly decorative trees don't know that the fruits are edible. To be sure, they won't convince anyone who eats one raw, right off the tree; they're quite bitter. But they make an interesting seasoning, and also can be juiced to make an unusual jelly.

Mountain ash are easy to gather in quantity; simply snip off the entire cluster. Wait until they are fully ripe before harvesting. Frost softens the berries and makes them a bit less bitter, so many foragers wait until after the first frost to harvest the fruit. They persist through the winter, and it's fun to trek through the woods on snowshoes to pick mountain ash. Harvested mountain ash fruits keep well in the refrigerator; simply place unwashed clusters—still on the stems—in a plastic bag. Twist the top just lightly, to allow some air to enter the bag, and refrigerate as long as 3 weeks. They also dehydrate well; see the instructions on pgs. 182–184.

Mountain ash trees grow in cool, moist, sun-dappled woods. They're an important winter food source for birds, bears and other wildlife.

To prepare juice from fresh mountain ash, pull individual fruits off the stems; discard any that are black, or withered and hard. Measure the picked fruit and place in a non-aluminum pot. Add 2 cups of water per 2 cups of picked fruit. Heat to boiling, then reduce the heat; cover and simmer for about 20 minutes. Gently mash the fruit with a potato masher, and cook for 5 minutes longer. Transfer the mixture to a strainer lined with doubled, dampened cheesecloth and let it drip for 30 minutes, pressing lightly to extract more juice. Processed this way, 2 cups of stemmed, fresh fruit will yield about 1 cup juice.

If you're preparing juice from dried mountain ash, follow the same instructions, increasing the water by half (so for 2 cups of dried mountain ash, you'd use 3 cups of water). Increase cooking time from 20 to 30 minutes.

Sweet Mountain Ash Jelly
2 half-pints

1½ cups mountain ash juice

One-third of a 1.75-ounce box powdered pectin

¼ teaspoon butter, optional (helps reduce foaming)

2 cups sugar

Prepare and process as directed in Jelly Instructions (using pectin), pg. 178.

Venison Roast with Mountain Ash and Juniper Rub

6 to 8 servings

Venison is a natural partner for mountain ash and juniper; both are part of the deer's diet.

Rub:

¼ cup mountain ash berries, crushed

6 juniper berries, crushed

1 teaspoon dried rosemary leaves, crushed

1 teaspoon dried thyme

1 teaspoon paprika

1 teaspoon salt

½ teaspoon freshly ground pepper

2- to 2½-pound venison roast from the hindquarter

2 tablespoons vegetable oil

1 medium onion, diced

1 cup dry red wine

½ cup sour cream

2 tablespoons currant jelly

2 teaspoons all-purpose flour

2 tablespoons cold water

In small bowl, combine all rub ingredients; mix well. Spread rub mixture on all sides of roast, pressing in. Place roast in plastic food-storage bag; seal and refrigerate overnight.

When you're ready to cook, heat oven to 350°F. In Dutch oven, heat oil over medium-high heat. Add roast; brown on all sides. Add onion and wine; cover and bake, basting occasionally, until desired doneness, 20 minutes per pound for rare and up to 30 minutes per pound for medium-well. Transfer roast to a serving plate; cover loosely with foil.

Strain pan juices through wire-mesh strainer into a bowl. Return juices to Dutch oven. Heat to boiling over medium-high heat. Reduce heat and boil gently until liquid is reduced to ¼ cup, 8 to 10 minutes. Stir in sour cream and jelly; cook until jelly melts. In small bowl, stir together flour and water; add to liquid in Dutch oven, stirring constantly. Cook until sauce is smooth and bubbling, 1 to 2 minutes. Serve sauce over sliced roast.

Substitution: Substitute a beef rump roast for the venison. Proceed as directed.

MULBERRIES *(Morus alba, M. rubra)*

There are two types of mulberries: white and red. Surprisingly, color of the ripe fruit is not the identifying factor. Some white mulberries are, indeed, whitish when ripe, but more commonly they are pink, red or deep purple; red mulberries are blackish when ripe. Both can be eaten raw or cooked; however, be sure that the fruit you pick is completely ripe and soft, as unripe fruit is not only hard and unpleasant but is also mildly toxic (as are the leaves and all other parts of the plant).

Mulberries are very common in urban areas, yet few people seem to pick them for eating. It's too bad, because the fruits are sweet and delicious—and if more folks were interested in picking them, there would be fewer mulberries staining the sidewalks!

The hardest part about picking mulberries is reaching the fruit, which is usually high up in the tree. The best way to harvest them is to spread a tarp under the tree, then jostle the branches with a stick; ripe fruit will fall onto the tarp and can be gathered. A short, soft stemlet remains attached to the fruit; this should be removed before eating or cooking the fruit. It's easiest to just pinch it off with your fingernails as you're washing the fruit.

To prepare pulp or juice, measure the fruit and place in a non-aluminum pot. For pulp, add ½ cup water per quart of fruit; for juice, add 1 cup water per quart of fruit. Thoroughly crush the fruit with a potato masher to start the juices flowing. Heat to boiling, then reduce the heat; cover and simmer for about 20 minutes. **For pulp,** the mixture is ready to use; you can also purée it in a food processor to make it smoother if you like. **For juice,** transfer the mixture to a strainer lined with doubled, dampened cheesecloth and let it drip for 30 minutes; if you're making jelly, don't squeeze the fruit or the jelly will be cloudy. After the clear liquid has dripped away, set it aside and squeeze the fruit into a different container; you can use this slightly cloudy juice as a beverage or for cooking, and add the leftover, squeezed fruit to applesauce, pie filling or other cooked fruits. Processed this way, a quart of fruit will yield about 1½ cups of pulp, or about 2 cups juice.

Once you've harvested mulberries, use them within a day or two, as they will spoil quickly. They freeze beautifully; simply pack them into containers or heavyweight plastic bags and freeze. They can be dried successfully (see pgs. 182–184); the texture of a dried mulberry is similar to that of a dried fig. Dried mulberries can be eaten out of hand as a nibble, or rehydrated in warm water and used like fresh berries.

Mulberry Thumbprint Cookies

About 28 cookies

Whole mulberries nestle inside a thumbprint pressed into a rich, buttery cookie.

½ cup (1 stick) unsalted butter, softened

¼ cup confectioners' sugar, plus additional for garnish

1½ teaspoons vanilla extract

1 cup all-purpose flour

¼ teaspoon salt

¼ cup very finely chopped pecans

¾ cup (approximate) fresh mulberries

In mixing bowl, combine butter, sugar and vanilla. Beat with electric mixer until light and fluffy, about 2 minutes; scrape bowl several times. Place a wire-mesh strainer over the mixing bowl; add flour and salt, then shake strainer to sift flour into the butter mixture. Add nuts. Stir with spatula or wooden spoon until well mixed. Cover and refrigerate for an hour (or longer); this makes the dough easy to handle.

When ready to bake, heat oven to 350°F. Roll chilled dough into balls that are about 1 inch in size. Place on ungreased baking sheet, about 1½ inches apart. Use your thumb to press a large indentation into the center of each ball. Place 3 or 4 mulberries (depending on size) into each indentation. Bake for 18 to 23 minutes, or until cookies are just set and are lightly golden brown. Remove baking sheet(s) from oven; use the back of a spoon to gently press each group of berries into the dough. Put a little confectioners' sugar into a wire-mesh strainer and shake it gently over the cookies to dust them lightly. Transfer to wire rack. Cool before serving.

Mulberry Jelly

4 half-pints

2¾ cups mulberry juice

2 tablespoons lemon juice

Two-thirds of a 1.75-ounce box powdered pectin

½ teaspoon butter, optional (helps reduce foaming)

3½ cups sugar

Prepare and process as directed in Jelly Instructions (using pectin), pg. 178.

Mulberry Ripple Cheesecake 1 cheesecake (10 to 12 servings)

This cheesecake is a great dessert for a large dinner party, and also works to take along to a potluck because it serves up to 12 people.

Crust:

¾ cup graham cracker crumbs

½ cup ground pecans

2 tablespoons white sugar

2 tablespoons (packed) golden brown sugar

4 tablespoons (half of a stick) butter, melted

Filling:

¾ cup smooth mulberry pulp (processed in blender)

2 tablespoons white sugar

1 teaspoon cornstarch

3 packages cream cheese (8 ounces each), softened

1 can (14 ounces) sweetened condensed milk

¼ cup freshly squeezed lemon juice

1 teaspoon vanilla extract

3 eggs, at room temperature

Heat oven to 350°F. Spray 9-inch springform pan (with removable edge) with nonstick spray. In mixing bowl, combine graham cracker crumbs, pecans, white sugar and brown sugar; stir to mix well. Drizzle butter over while stirring; continue stirring until well mixed. Pour into prepared pan; use a small glass to firmly press the crumbs evenly into the pan and about 1 inch up the sides. Bake until light golden brown, 10 to 12 minutes. Transfer to a wire rack; let cool while you prepare the filling. Reduce oven to 300°F.

For the filling: Combine mulberry pulp and sugar in small saucepan. Heat over medium heat, stirring constantly, until sugar dissolves, about 3 minutes. Stir in cornstarch. Increase heat to medium-high and cook, stirring frequently, until mixture thickens, about 1 minute. Remove from heat and cool slightly, then pour into a measuring cup that has a spout and place in freezer to chill for a few minutes.

In large mixing bowl, beat cream cheese with electric mixer until light and fluffy, about 2 minutes. Gradually add condensed milk, beating constantly and scraping the sides of the bowl as necessary. Add lemon juice and vanilla; beat until well mixed. Add eggs, one at a time, beating well after each addition.

Pour cream cheese mixture into crust, spreading evenly. Drizzle the mulberry mixture over the top, pouring in several thin circles to form a bull's-eye pattern. Swirl a table knife through the circles to create a ripple effect; don't let the knife go all the way down to the crust. Bake until cheesecake is puffy around the edges but still a bit loose in the center, 50 to 60 minutes. Transfer to a wire rack; set aside to cool completely. Wrap tightly with plastic wrap or foil, and refrigerate at least 8 hours or overnight.

To serve, run a sharp knife around the edge of the pan to loosen the cake, then carefully remove the ring around the edge. Cut into thin slices; if the knife is sticking, dip it into hot water and dry quickly before continuing.

Variation: Substitute 1 cup raspberry or blackberry purée for the mulberry pulp; increase cornstarch to 1½ teaspoons. Because this purée is a bit thinner than the mulberry pulp, it needs a bit more cooking time to reduce it before adding the cornstarch.

 Note that the cheesecake must be prepared at least a half-day in advance; overnight is better, to give the cheesecake time to firm and allow the flavors to meld.

Mulberry Filling
About ½ cup; easily increased

½ teaspoon water

½ teaspoon cornstarch

5 ounces mulberries (about 1 cup)

1 tablespoon grated apple

2 teaspoons sugar

1½ teaspoons lemon juice

In small bowl, blend together water and cornstarch; set aside. In small, heavy-bottomed saucepan, combine mulberries, apple, sugar and lemon juice. Crush fruit gently with a potato masher to start juices flowing. Heat to boiling over medium-high heat, then cook, stirring frequently, until mixture is no longer runny; this will take 10 to 12 minutes. Add cornstarch mixture, stirring constantly; cook for about 1 minute longer, or until thick. Cool before using.

Use this to prepare Easy Bear Claws (pg. 30), Fruit-Striped Cookie Fingers (pg. 145), or Fruit-Filled Muffins (pg. 163). Refrigerate extra filling, and use to top oatmeal or toast.

Mulberry-Rhubarb Pie with Crumble Topping
1 pie (6 to 8 servings)

Rhubarb adds a nice touch of tartness and complexity to the mulberries, which are quite sweet on their own. It also happens to be in season when mulberries are ripe, making this a perfect combination.

Crumble topping:

4 tablespoons (half of a stick) cold unsalted butter

⅔ cup all-purpose flour

¼ cup (packed) light brown sugar

3 tablespoons white sugar

¼ teaspoon cinnamon

A pinch of salt

Ready-to-use pastry for single-crust pie

¾ cup sugar

3 tablespoons quick-cooking tapioca

2 cups fresh rhubarb, cut into ½-inch chunks before measuring

1½ cups fresh mulberries

2 tablespoons unsalted butter, cut into bits

½ teaspoon vanilla extract

Heat oven to 400°F. Prepare crumble topping: Cut butter into ½-inch cubes and combine in food processor with remaining topping ingredients. Pulse for a few short bursts, just until mixture resembles coarse meal. Transfer to a bowl and refrigerate until needed; don't wash the food processor, as you'll need it in the next step.

Fit pastry into pie plate, then turn under and crimp edges; set aside. In food processor, combine sugar and tapioca; process for 15 seconds (this makes the tapioca finer, so it cooks more evenly). Pour into large mixing bowl. Add rhubarb, mulberries, butter and vanilla; stir gently. Spoon evenly into crust. Use a spoon to sprinkle crumble topping evenly over filling. Place pie on a baking sheet (to catch drips) and bake in the lower third of the oven for 30 minutes. Reduce heat to 350°F, and bake for 30 minutes longer, until topping is nicely browned and filling is bubbly. Cool on a rack for 2 hours before serving.

Rice Pudding with Wild Berries

Tender, custardy rice pudding is studded with colorful fruits.

1 tablespoon butter, softened

2¾ cups whole milk

6 egg yolks

¾ cup sugar

½ teaspoon vanilla extract

½ teaspoon lemon extract

1 teaspoon cinnamon

⅛ teaspoon salt

4 cups cooked long-grain rice (from about 1½ cups raw rice)

1 cup mulberries, raspberries or blackberries, cut in half if long

Heat oven to 350°F. Generously butter 9-inch-square baking dish; set aside. In saucepan, heat milk over medium heat until small bubbles appear around the edges; remove from heat. In large mixing bowl, use a whisk to beat egg yolks and sugar until light. Add warm milk, vanilla and lemon extracts, cinnamon and salt; whisk to blend. Add rice and stir with a wooden spoon until well mixed. Add mulberries; stir gently to mix. Scrape mixture into prepared dish. Bake until lightly browned on top, 40 to 50 minutes. Cool for 5 to 10 minutes, and serve while still warm.

Other recipes in this book featuring mulberries:
Six Recipes Using Wild Fruit Juice or Syrup, pgs. 172–176
Wild Berry or Fruit Syrup, pg. 177
Dehydrating Wild Berries and Fruits, pgs. 182–184
Wild Berry or Fruit Leather, pg. 184

Quick ideas for using mulberries:
Mix a few into any baking recipe that uses raspberries. The mulberries have a more solid texture and are generally a bit larger than raspberries, so they should be cut into two shorter halves if longer than ¾ inch to make them more similar to the raspberries.

MUSCADINES *(Vitis rotundifolia)*

Muscadines are North America's largest native wild grape, up to an inch across with speckled skin. They grow on long, climbing vines that often reach high into trees, draping over the branches. Not all fruits in a cluster ripen at the same time, so when picking, choose only the ripe ones. If you can't reach the fruit to pick it, place a drop cloth on the ground, then jostle the vine with a pole; ripe muscadines fall off easily.

A bronze variety of muscadine, called "scuppernong," is cultivated for wine-making and eating; bronze muscadines are occasionally found in the wild.

Muscadine skin is tough and leathery, and often slightly bitter. Some old-time recipes call for boiling muscadine skins until tender, then using them to make a pie. I haven't tried this, but if you have a pile of skins, give it a try. Muscadines don't keep well; the break in the skin where the stem was attached is large, and the fruit spoils quickly. Keep muscadines refrigerated, and use in a few days.

Like other wild grapes, muscadines contain tartrate (see pg. 70). Muscadines, however, contain far less than most, and many cooks make jelly from the juice without worrying about the tartrate. I've never had a tartrate problem when eating raw muscadines or cooking with them, but I do settle the juice before making jelly so it will be clearer.

To prepare juice, cut each fruit in half. Pick out the seeds with the knife tip, then add the muscadine half to a food processor. As you add each half, hold it over the workbowl and stick your thumb firmly into the cavity to check for seeds, letting the juice drip into the workbowl. Chop the fruit to medium texture. Measure the chopped fruit, then transfer to a non-aluminum pot; for each cup of chopped fruit, add ⅓ cup water. Heat over medium heat until mixture just begins to boil, then reduce heat, cover and simmer for 15 minutes, stirring occasionally. Transfer to a strainer lined with doubled, dampened cheesecloth and let it drip for 30 minutes; if you're making jelly, don't squeeze the fruit or the jelly will be cloudy. After the liquid has dripped away, set it aside and squeeze the fruit into a different container. Processed this way, 1½ pounds of muscadines will yield about 1¾ cups clear juice and ½ cup cloudy juice which can be used as a beverage or for cooking.

To settle out the tartrate, place the juice, covered, in the refrigerator for 24 to 48 hours; a sediment will develop. Carefully pour the clear juice into a clean jar; pour slowly to avoid stirring the sediment up, and as soon as it nears the stream of liquid you're pouring, stop.

To remove seeds and skin so the fruit can be used in recipes, cut a muscadine in half from top to bottom. Use a grapefruit spoon (a serrated-tip teaspoon) to pick out the seeds. Now slide the spoon between the flesh and the skin, going all the way to the bottom of flesh but not through the skin. Rotate the fruit, keeping the spoon tightly against the skin; after a full rotation, the flesh will pop out cleanly. Hold each skinned half up to the light so you can see any shadows that reveal a seed you might have missed. If the fruit is discolored at the stem end, slice off and discard the darkened part. Working this way, I can do a pound of muscadines in about 30 minutes; I typically get about 1½ cups of seedless, skinned muscadine halves per pound of whole fruit.

Muscadine Bars

This is a soft bar cookie, almost cake-like. They keep for several days at room temperature.

1 pound whole muscadines

5 tablespoons unsalted butter, softened, divided

2 tablespoons dried cranberries (craisins)

1 tablespoon freshly squeezed lemon juice

4 ounces cream cheese, softened

¾ cup (packed) brown sugar

½ teaspoon vanilla extract

1 egg

1¼ cups all-purpose flour

½ teaspoon baking soda

½ teaspoon salt

¼ cup old-fashioned rolled oats

¼ cup chopped pecans or other nuts

Cut muscadines in half and remove seeds and skin as directed on pg. 104. Cut each seedless half into 3 pieces by placing them, cut-side down, on cutting board and slicing straight down; you will end up with 1⅓ to 1½ cups of half-round slices that are about ¼ inch thick. Melt 1 tablespoon of the butter in medium skillet over medium heat. Add muscadines and any juice from the measuring cup; stir in cranberries and lemon juice. Cook without stirring until juices have mostly cooked away, then cook, stirring occasionally, until muscadine slices are beginning to brown slightly; total cooking time is about 10 minutes. Remove from heat and set aside to cool slightly.

Heat oven to 350°F. Spray 8-inch-square baking dish with nonstick spray; set aside. In mixing bowl, combine cream cheese and remaining ¼ cup butter; beat until creamy with electric mixer. Add brown sugar and vanilla; beat until smooth. Add egg; beat until combined. Place a wire-mesh strainer on a dinner plate. Add flour, baking soda and salt; shake strainer over mixing bowl to sift into cream cheese mixture. Beat on low speed until combined.

Press about two-thirds of the dough into prepared pan, smoothing with a wet rubber spatula or damp fingers. Spread muscadine mixture evenly over the top. Add oats and nuts to remaining dough; stir with a wooden spoon to mix well. Drop by heaping teaspoons on top of fruit; there will be some gaps between the topping. Bake until topping is golden brown, 25 to 30 minutes. Transfer to wire rack to cool completely before cutting.

Mediterranean Chicken with Muscadines
6 servings

The sunny flavors of the Mediterranean—onions, garlic, olives and roasted red peppers—combine with muscadines for a delightful dish. Serve over buttered noodles.

1 medium yellow or white onion, halved and thinly sliced

3 cloves garlic, thinly sliced

1 bay leaf

8 ounces whole muscadines

3 bone-in, skin-on chicken breast halves (about 3 pounds total)

1½ tablespoons olive oil

Salt and freshly ground pepper

½ teaspoon paprika (smoked paprika is really good here)

1 jar (7 to 7.5 ounces) roasted red bell peppers, drained

¾ cup white wine or chicken broth

2 tablespoons (packed) brown sugar

1 tablespoon lemon juice

½ cup pitted, halved green Spanish olives

2 tablespoons coarsely chopped fresh basil

1 tablespoon coarsely chopped fresh Italian (flat-leaf) parsley

Heat oven to 425°F. Scatter onion, garlic and bay leaf in the bottom of a Dutch oven. Cut muscadines in half and remove seeds (but leave the skin on); scatter halved muscadines over the onions. Cut each chicken breast half crosswise into 2 pieces; place over muscadines, skin-side up. Drizzle olive oil over the chicken; sprinkle with salt and pepper to taste, then with the paprika. Bake, uncovered, for 25 minutes. While chicken is baking, cut drained roasted peppers into ½-inch-wide strips. Combine wine, brown sugar and lemon juice in measuring cup.

When chicken has baked for 25 minutes, remove from oven. Scatter roasted peppers and olives over chicken; pour wine mixture into pan. Return to oven; reduce heat to 375°F. Bake for 30 to 35 minutes longer, basting several times, until juices from chicken run clear. Remove from oven and let stand for 5 minutes, then scatter basil and parsley over everything before serving.

 Weighing is the best way to measure muscadines; because of their large size, they don't pack well into a measuring cup (especially a small one).

Tangy Muscadine Barbecue Sauce   About 3 cups sauce

This sauce has a pleasant kick to it; the muscadines add sweetness and a chunky texture.

3 cloves garlic

Half of a fresh jalapeño, seeds removed

Half of a medium onion, cut into 1-inch chunks

¾ pound whole muscadines (about 2½ cups, measured in a 1-quart measuring cup)

1½ cups ketchup

½ cup apple cider

½ cup (packed) brown sugar

2 tablespoons rice vinegar or white vinegar

1 tablespoon soy sauce

1 teaspoon smoked or regular (sweet) paprika

1 teaspoon dry mustard powder

½ teaspoon freshly ground black pepper

In food processor, mince garlic and jalapeño. Add onion; pulse a few times. Cut muscadines in half and remove seeds (but leave the skin on), then add to food processor; as you add each half, stick your thumb firmly into the cavity to check for seeds. Process until muscadines are finely chopped. Transfer mixture to heavy-bottomed non-aluminum saucepan; add remaining ingredients. Heat until mixture just boils, then reduce heat and simmer, stirring frequently, for 45 minutes, or until desired consistency.

Muscadine Filling   About ½ cup; easily increased

1 cup seedless, skinless muscadine halves (from about ¾ pound whole fruit; see pg. 104)

½ teaspoon cornstarch

In food processor, chop muscadine halves until fine. Transfer to a small saucepan; stir in cornstarch. Cook over medium-low heat, stirring constantly, until thickened, about 3 minutes. Cool before using.

Use this to prepare Easy Bear Claws (pg. 30), Fruit-Striped Cookie Fingers (pg. 145), or Fruit-Filled Muffins (pg. 163). Refrigerate extra filling, and use to top oatmeal or toast.

Muscadine Tart

This is a very impressive-looking dessert that is surprisingly easy to put together. It's awesome served warm, with a scoop of vanilla-bean ice cream on each serving.

1 sheet frozen puff pastry (half of 17.3-ounce package), thawed as directed

1 egg, lightly beaten

16 whole muscadines

2 tablespoons plus 1 teaspoon muscadine or currant jelly

1 slightly heaping tablespoon coarse sugar such as turbinado

Note: You may prepare the crust and muscadines several hours in advance, then refrigerate them, separately, until you are ready to bake. When you're ready, heat the oven; when it is at the proper temperature, assemble the tart and bake immediately. If you want to do it all at once, follow the instructions below.

Line baking sheet with cooking parchment. Cut a 2-inch strip off the end of the still-folded puff pastry. Unfold the larger portion of the pastry onto the parchment. Unfold the smaller strip of pastry next to one of the narrow edges; trim the thin strip so it is the same width as the rest of the pastry (the final pastry should be about 7½ inches wide and 11½ inches long). Use your fingers to pinch the edges together where the thin strip butts against the larger piece, then press gently with a fork. Carefully turn the pastry over and seal the seam on the second side. Brush egg over 1 inch of the pastry edge on all sides. Fold a scant inch of the pastry over on all sides to make a border; press to seal. With a small knife, cut ½-inch-long slits around the entire edge, spacing the slits ½ inch apart and cutting completely through pastry. Prick the flat center of the pastry all over with a fork. Cover with waxed paper and refrigerate while you prepare the muscadines.

When you are ready to bake, start heating the oven to 400°F. Line a plate with several layers of paper towels. Cut the muscadines in half and remove the seeds and skin as directed on pg. 104, placing each seedless, skinless half, cut-side down, on the paper towel-lined plate. Set aside until oven is ready.

When the oven is ready, assemble the tart: Spread jelly evenly over the center of the pastry, keeping it off the raised edges. Pat top sides of muscadine halves gently with paper towels. Arrange 8 muscadine halves, cut-side down, in a row along one long edge, butting the fruit up to the pastry edge. Add 3 more rows, arranging the fruit neatly and evenly. Sprinkle sugar evenly over muscadines. Bake tart in the center of the oven for 35 to 40 minutes; edges should be nicely browned but not burned. Let cool for at least 20 minutes before serving. To serve, cut tart crosswise into 4 strips (with 2 rows of fruit per strip); for smaller servings, cut each strip into 2 shorter halves (each with 4 muscadine halves). This tart is best served the day it is made.

Pork Tenderloin with Caramelized Muscadines
4 servings

Be sure to have the muscadines seeded and skinned, and the shallots chopped, before you start cooking the tenderloin; you won't have time to prep them once cooking has started.

½ teaspoon dry mustard powder

½ teaspoon paprika (smoked paprika is very good)

½ teaspoon crumbled dried thyme leaves

¼ teaspoon salt

¼ teaspoon coarsely ground black pepper

¼ teaspoon ground ginger

1 pork tenderloin (about 1 pound), cut into 2 halves

2 teaspoons olive oil

1½ teaspoons unsalted butter

1½ cups seedless, skinless muscadine halves (from about 1 pound whole fruit; see pg. 104)

2 large shallots, minced

½ cup chicken broth

1 teaspoon Dijon mustard

Heat oven to 375°F. In a small bowl, combine mustard powder, paprika, thyme, salt, pepper and ginger; mix well. Sprinkle spice blend over pork, rubbing it in with your fingertips.

Heat oil in large, heavy-bottomed skillet over medium heat until shimmering. Add pork, and cook for about 3 minutes, until nicely brown. Turn and brown the other side. Transfer to a baking dish that holds the pork comfortably; bake, uncovered, for 20 to 25 minutes, or until center reads 145°F on an instant-read thermometer.

As soon as you get the pork in the oven, start preparing the sauce: In same skillet, melt butter over medium heat. Add muscadines, stirring to coat. Cook, stirring occasionally, until juices released from muscadines cook away and muscadines are slightly caramelized, about 12 minutes. Add shallots; cook and stir for about 2 minutes longer. Add broth and Dijon mustard; increase heat to high and cook, stirring frequently, until mixture is saucelike, about 3 minutes. Set aside and keep warm until pork is ready.

When pork reads 145°F, remove from oven; cover loosely with foil and set aside for 5 minutes (the internal temperature of the pork will rise during this time). Slice pork across the grain into ¾-inch-thick slices; serve with muscadine sauce.

Muscadine-Apple Pandowdy

This rustic skillet pie is gorgeous, with caramelized juices peeking out of the browned crust.

¾ cup apple cider

¼ cup (packed) golden brown sugar

1 tablespoon freshly squeezed lemon juice

2 teaspoons cornstarch

¼ teaspoon salt

2 tablespoons butter

1½ cups seedless, skinless muscadine halves (from about 1 pound whole fruit; see pg. 104)

2 Granny Smith or other tart apples (about 1 pound), peeled, cored and cubed (½-inch cubes)

Ready-to-use pastry for single-crust pie

1 egg white, beaten

1 tablespoon white sugar

Position oven rack in top third of oven; heat to 450°F. In small bowl, stir together cider, brown sugar, lemon juice, cornstarch and salt; set aside. In heavy, oven-safe 10-inch skillet, melt butter over medium heat. Add muscadine halves. Cook without stirring until juices released by muscadines have mostly cooked away, then cook, stirring occasionally, until muscadines are beginning to brown nicely; total cooking time is about 10 minutes. Add apples; cook for 5 minutes longer, stirring several times. Stir cider mixture again, then pour into skillet; stir to combine, then remove from heat. Level fruit with a spoon; working carefully to avoid burning yourself, place pastry on top of fruit, using a spoon to tuck pastry edges down along the inside edge of the skillet. Brush pastry with egg white; sprinkle with white sugar. Use a sharp knife to make 4 cuts in the pastry in a tic-tac-toe pattern; as you cut, the pastry edges will be partially pushed down into the pan juices. Place skillet on top rack and bake until crust is rich golden brown and juices are bubbling, 20 to 25 minutes. Let cool on wire rack for 15 minutes before serving.

Lower-Sugar Muscadine Jelly
3 half-pints

This is a gorgeous, rosy-purple jelly with an intriguing flavor that is unmistakably "grape," but more subtle than other wild grape jellies or commercial grape jelly. Muscadines are sweeter than most wild grapes; the use of special lower-sugar pectin allows the natural flavor of the muscadines to really shine.

1¼ cups sugar

Half of a 1.75-ounce box powdered Sure-Jell® Premium Pectin for Less or No Sugar Needed Recipes

½ cup water

1²/₃ cups muscadine juice

Sterilize 3 half-pint jars, bands and lids as directed on pg. 185, or have 3 half-pint plastic freezer jelly containers ready (pg. 162). In medium non-aluminum saucepan, stir together sugar and pectin until well mixed. Stir in water. Heat to boiling over medium-high heat, stirring constantly. Cook at a full boil for 1 minute, stirring constantly. Remove from heat. Immediately add muscadine juice; stir for 1 minute, or until thoroughly mixed. Pour into prepared jars (or containers), leaving ½ inch headspace; cover with clean lids. Let stand at room temperature for 24 hours; the jelly should be set. If it is not set, refrigerate for several days until set before freezing; it may take a few days to set. The jelly will keep for 3 weeks in the refrigerator, or it may be frozen for up to a year.

Other recipes in this book featuring muscadines:
    Wild Grape-Black Cherry Wine, pg. 72
    Six Recipes Using Wild Fruit Juice or Syrup, pgs. 172–176
    Wild Berry or Fruit Syrup, pg. 177
    Dehydrating Wild Berries and Fruits, pgs. 182–184

Quick ideas for using muscadines:
    Add some seedless, skinless muscadine halves to chicken salad; the flavor
        combination is fabulous.
    Substitute 1 to 1½ cups of seedless, skinless muscadine halves for some of the
        apple when making an apple pie.

PAWPAWS *(Asimina triloba)*

Pawpaws are a favorite of foragers; they are also sold occasionally at farmers' markets and grocery stores. Their soft, creamy flesh has a definite tropical taste; it's a bit like mixing bananas with pineapples and a touch of apricot. Ripe pawpaws are slightly soft to the touch, and often have black blotches on the skin. Slightly underripe pawpaws will ripen if left at room temperature for a few days, but the flavor is not as good as that of tree-ripened fruits. Overripe pawpaws have red blotches in the flesh, and should not be used.

Pawpaws can be eaten raw, right from the shell, but are more often peeled, mashed and used in baked goods. They contain numerous large, flat, inedible seeds, which must be removed before mashing the fruit.

Pawpaws are featured in at least two popular songs. "Way Down Yonder in the Pawpaw Patch" is a well-known song often taught to young children; the "Pawpaw Tree" song is much less known, and has very odd lyrics indeed!

No matter how you do it, processing pawpaws is a messy job. The traditional method is to cut the pawpaw open and scoop out the soft flesh with a spoon, then pick out the seeds and scrape the flesh off them; finally, the flesh is mashed with a potato masher. I've also had good luck pushing a quartered pawpaw, cut side down, into a wire-mesh strainer set over a large bowl; after the pawpaw flesh breaks apart and goes through the strainer, I rub the skin and the seeds against the strainer to rasp off as much flesh as possible. The strainer method produces silky-smooth purée; if you prefer chunky pulp, use the traditional method instead. Note that if you try to cut a pawpaw lengthwise, the knife will run into the seeds, but you can cut between the seeds if you cut the fruit crosswise. An average 7- to 8-ounce pawpaw will yield about ½ cup of mashed or strained pulp, as well as a pile of inedible seeds; most sources say that pawpaws have 8 to 13 seeds, but I once counted 16 seeds from a single bruiser as I was cleaning it.

For pawpaw slices, use a very sharp paring knife to peel the pawpaw as closely as possible. Lay the peeled pawpaw on a cutting board, and slice off ¼-inch-thick pieces of the fruit, turning it as you go; the slices will look like half-moons, and are typically 1 to 1½ inches long and about half as wide. When you encounter a seed, slice alongside it on both sides to separate it from the rest of the fruit; cut off whatever flesh is still attached to the seed, and keep working on the rest of the fruit. Yield will depend on the size of the pawpaw (and your knife skills); typically, you'll get ½ cup of slices from a 7- to 8-ounce pawpaw, plus some bits of fruit that are too small to use as slices, but can be mashed.

Mashed or strained pawpaw pulp freezes quite well; simply pack a measured amount into a freezer-safe container, label with the quantity, and seal tightly. It can be kept for several months with no loss of quality, as long as the container has an air-tight seal.

Some people get digestive upset from pawpaws; underripe and overripe pawpaws are particularly problematical, and should not be eaten. If you're eating pawpaws for the first time, start with a small quantity, to be sure you won't have any problems.

Pawpaw-Buttermilk Muffins

12 muffins

The pawpaw flavor really comes through in these moist, tender muffins. They're great warm, but will keep at room temperature, well wrapped, for several days. Refrigerate or freeze for longer storage.

1½ cups all-purpose flour

½ cup sugar

1½ teaspoons baking powder

¼ teaspoon baking soda

¼ teaspoon salt

⅛ teaspoon nutmeg

¾ cup buttermilk

1 egg

6 tablespoons unsalted butter, melted and cooled

¾ cup mashed pawpaw

1 tablespoon turbinado or other coarse sugar, optional

Heat oven to 375°F. Line a 12-cup muffin tin with papers, or coat with nonstick spray. Place a wire-mesh strainer over a large mixing bowl. Add flour, sugar, baking powder, baking soda, salt and nutmeg; shake strainer to sift into bowl. In measuring cup or a small bowl, beat together buttermilk and egg with a fork. Add the buttermilk mixture to the flour mixture; fold together with a rubber spatula until the dry ingredients are just moistened. Fold in the melted butter, then add the pawpaw and fold in; don't over-mix or the muffins will be tough. Gently spoon the mixture into the prepared muffin tin. Sprinkle the tops with coarse sugar, if using. Bake until muffins are golden brown and the tops spring back when pressed lightly, 25 to 30 minutes. Place muffin tin on cooling rack for about 5 minutes, then remove muffins from tin and let cool completely on wire rack.

Pawpaw-Stuffed French Toast   2 servings; easily increased

Here's a fun way to serve pawpaws for breakfast. The sandwiches are started in a skillet, and finish cooking in the oven. Serve with some orange juice and bacon, if you like; you'll have time to cook the bacon while the sandwiches are in the oven.

½ cup whole milk

2 eggs

¼ teaspoon cinnamon

1 average-sized pawpaw, or ¼ cup mashed pawpaw

4 slices sandwich bread (see below)

1½ teaspoons honey

2 teaspoons butter or margarine

Heat oven to 375°F. Choose a baking dish that is large enough to hold the sandwiches in a single layer; coat with nonstick spray and set aside. In measuring cup or small bowl, beat together milk, eggs and cinnamon with a fork; set aside. Peel the pawpaw, and cut off as many slices as you can. Spread one side of each bread slice with honey, dividing evenly. Arrange a layer of pawpaw slices on top of two of the slices; cover the bread but don't overlap too much or double up the pawpaw slices (the sandwiches won't cook properly if the pawpaw is too thick). Refrigerate any remaining pawpaw for another use. (If using mashed pawpaw, simply spread it over two slices.) Top with remaining bread, putting the honey-spread side to the inside. Pour half of the milk mixture into a flat-bottomed baking dish. Place the sandwiches in the milk side by side; pour remaining milk mixture over. Let stand for 5 to 10 minutes.

In a large skillet, melt the butter over medium heat. Use a spatula to transfer the soaked sandwiches to the skillet, placing them in a single layer. Cook for 2 minutes, then turn carefully and cook for one minute longer. Transfer to prepared baking dish. Bake for 18 minutes; the bread should be puffy. Serve immediately.

 Sandwich bread is slightly thinner, and a bit firmer, than regular commercial sliced bread; the slices are square rather than rounded on top. I use Pepperidge Farm Sandwich White for this recipe. Regular commercial sliced bread will work, but it might have a tendency to fall apart because it may get too mushy during the soaking.

Pawpaw-Oatmeal-Butterscotch Cookies About 30

Butterscotch is a nice flavor to pair with pawpaws; oatmeal and nuts add a pleasing texture to these soft, tender cookies.

½ cup (1 stick) unsalted butter, softened

⅓ cup (packed) brown sugar

⅓ cup white sugar

½ cup mashed pawpaw

1 egg

1 teaspoon vanilla extract

1¼ cups all-purpose flour

½ teaspoon baking soda

½ teaspoon salt

1 cup quick-cooking oatmeal (not instant)

⅓ cup butterscotch morsels

Heat oven to 375°F. Line two baking sheets with kitchen parchment, or coat with non-stick spray; set aside. In mixing bowl, beat butter, brown sugar and white sugar with an electric hand mixer until creamy. Add pawpaw, egg and vanilla; beat until smooth.

Place a wire-mesh strainer over the mixing bowl (or on a plate). Add flour, baking soda and salt; shake to sift into pawpaw mixture. Stir with a wooden spoon until just moistened. Add oatmeal and butterscotch chips; stir to combine. Drop by heaping tablespoons onto prepared baking sheet. Bake until golden brown and somewhat springy to the touch, 14 to 16 minutes; rotate pans once (see "Rotating Cookies while Baking," pg. 15). Remove baking sheets from oven and let cool for several minutes, then transfer cookies to wire racks and let cool completely.

Look for butterscotch morsels with the chocolate chips in the baking aisle.

Pawpaw Slices on Coconut Sticky Rice

4 servings

Serve this warm, sweet-but-not-too-sweet dish for dessert, or as part of a brunch menu. It's based on a classic Thai dish which pairs mangoes with sticky rice.

1 cup uncooked sweet rice (see below)

¾ cup unsweetened canned coconut milk

3 tablespoons sugar

2 or 3 ripe pawpaws, depending on size

2 to 3 tablespoons shredded or flaked coconut, optional

Rinse the sweet rice in a wire-mesh strainer. Place in a large mixing bowl. Add enough cold water to cover the rice by 2 inches. Let the rice soak at room temperature for at least 4 hours, and as long as overnight (cover the bowl with a plate or some foil if soaking overnight).

When you're ready to cook the rice, line the bottom of a bamboo steamer (or vegetable steamer) with a paper coffee filter or cheesecloth. Drain the sweet rice, then spoon evenly into the steamer. Cover the steamer tightly and place over boiling water. Steam for 20 minutes, or until the rice is cooked through but still chewy. Near the end of cooking time, combine coconut milk and sugar in a heavy-bottomed saucepan. Heat over medium-high heat, stirring frequently, until sugar has dissolved and milk has reduced a bit. Transfer the cooked rice to the saucepan with the coconut milk; stir well. Cook for 2 or 3 minutes, stirring constantly. Cover and remove from heat; set aside while you prepare the pawpaws.

Slice the pawpaws as directed on pg. 112; you need 1 to 1¼ cups pawpaw slices for this recipe. Divide the warm rice evenly between 4 serving bowls (if serving on a brunch table, pile all the rice onto a deep serving plate). Top with pawpaw slices; sprinkle with coconut.

Variation: Substitute 1 heaping tablespoon of coconut cream (used for specialty cocktails; Coco Casa is a common brand) for the coconut milk and sugar. You don't need to cook the coconut cream; simply stir it into the just-cooked rice and serve.

Sticky rice is a Thai specialty; when cooked, it's very sticky but not gummy. The uncooked rice is usually called sweet or glutinous rice; it's found in Asian specialty stores, and, increasingly, in large supermarkets. If you can't find it, use 2½ cups steamed sushi rice or short-grain rice (the kind used for risotto). Note that the sticky rice requires lengthy soaking, so plan ahead.

Frozen Pawpaw Delights

This is a fun way to serve pawpaw—guaranteed to please even the kids!

1 cup semi-sweet chocolate chips

1 tablespoon vegetable oil

1 ripe pawpaw (7 to 8 ounces)

1 cup (approx.) crushed pretzels, or finely chopped nuts

In small, heavy-bottomed saucepan, combine chocolate chips and oil. Heat over low heat, stirring almost constantly, until chips melt completely. Remove from heat and set aside to cool for 5 to 8 minutes.

While the chocolate is cooling, peel the pawpaw and cut into wedge-shaped slices as described on pg. 112; try to keep the pieces as large and uniform as possible. Line a baking sheet with waxed paper; place the crushed pretzels (or nuts) in a wide, flat bowl.

When chocolate is just warm but no longer hot, place a pawpaw slice in the pan and turn it carefully with a fork; don't pierce the pawpaw slice, just use the fork to move it around. Remove the pawpaw from the chocolate, letting the excess chocolate drip back into the pan. Place the chocolate-dipped slice into the bowl with the pretzels or nuts; use a clean spoon to sprinkle some of the topping on the top side of the pawpaw. Use a clean fork to lift the pawpaw out of the topping, and place it onto the wax paper-lined baking sheet. Repeat with remaining pawpaw slices, placing them on the baking sheet so they don't touch. Place the baking sheet into the freezer; freeze for at least 2 hours before serving. Leftovers can be kept in the freezer for several weeks in an air-tight freezer container; place a piece of waxed paper between layers. Serve frozen.

Pawpaw Colada

If you enjoy tropical cocktails, try this delightful blend.

¼ cup mashed ripe pawpaw

½ cup pineapple juice

3 tablespoons (1 jigger) dark rum, or to taste

1 tablespoon coconut cream (used for specialty cocktails)

½ cup ice cubes

In blender, combine pawpaw, pineapple juice, rum, cream of coconut and ice cubes. Blend at high speed until smooth and creamy. Pour drink into a chilled glass; serve.

Pawpaw Fritters

Serve these puffy, golden fritters for dessert, or as a warm, sweet snack. They would also be wonderful on a brunch table.

1 egg

⅔ cup cold cream

½ cup all-purpose flour

2 tablespoons (packed) brown sugar

⅛ teaspoon baking soda

1 to 2 tablespoons of cold water

½ cup pawpaw slices

Peanut oil for frying

Confectioners' sugar for dusting

In a mixing bowl, combine egg, cream, flour, brown sugar and baking soda. Beat with a fork until smooth, then beat in cold water, a bit at a time, until the mixture is loose enough for coating but not runny; it should be like thick pancake batter. Add the pawpaw slices and stir gently.

In a deep, heavy saucepan, heat 1 inch of oil to 375°F. With a fork, remove a few pawpaw slices, letting excess batter drain back into bowl. Place the slices, with the batter that clings to them, on a tablespoon and carefully drop the contents of the spoon into the oil. Repeat with two more batches, so you will be frying three fritters at a time. Fry until rich golden brown, turning once; this will take about a minute. Remove with a slotted spoon and transfer to a paper towel-lined plate. Repeat with remaining pawpaw slices. Dust with confectioners' sugar and serve warm.

Other recipes in this book using pawpaws:
Easy Bear Claws, pg. 30
Fruit-Filled Muffins, pg. 163
As a variation in Persimmon Smoothie, pg. 131

Quick ideas for using pawpaws:
Substitute mashed pawpaws for mashed bananas in muffins, quick breads and other baked goods; they also work well as banana substitute in smoothies.

PEACHES *(Prunus persica)*

While not common in our area, peaches are occasionally found growing wild. The fruits tend to be quite a bit smaller than orchard-grown peaches, and the skin might be pale in color rather than the yellowish-orange we're used to seeing. Like many wild fruits, eating quality varies quite a bit from tree to tree. Some are sweet and delicious, and taste even better than store-bought peaches; use these in the same way that you would use commercially grown peaches. Others are almost bitter in flavor; these work well for pickling.

Peach Filling   About ½ cup; easily increased

½ teaspoon water

¼ teaspoon cornstarch

¾ cup finely chopped peaches, peeled before chopping

1 tablespoon sugar, or as needed according to the sweetness of the fruit

½ teaspoon lemon juice

¼ teaspoon vanilla extract

In small bowl, blend together water and cornstarch; set aside. In small, heavy-bottomed saucepan, combine chopped peaches, 1 tablespoon sugar, the lemon juice and vanilla. Heat to boiling over medium-high heat, then cook, stirring frequently, until fruit is soft and is beginning to break up; this will take 5 to 10 minutes. Taste, and add additional sugar if necessary; cook for a minute longer, stirring constantly to dissolve the sugar. Add cornstarch mixture, stirring constantly; cook for 1 to 2 minutes longer, or until thick. Cool before using.

Use this to prepare Easy Bear Claws (pg. 30), Fruit-Striped Cookie Fingers (pg. 145), or Fruit-Filled Muffins (pg. 163). Refrigerate extra filling, and use to top oatmeal or toast.

Sweet-Sour Pickled Peaches

Serve these as a side dish with ham and other smoked meats; I've also read that some people enjoy them on cucumber sandwiches. Try it and see what you think!

About 2 pounds wild peaches

1½ cups sugar

¾ cup apple cider vinegar

⅓ cup water

4 whole cloves

1 whole cinnamon stick

Sterilize a wide-mouth pint canning jar, band and new lid according to the instructions on pg. 185; let the jar sit in the hot water until needed. Peel the peaches by placing them, a few at a time, into a saucepan of boiling water for about a minute; remove with a slotted spoon and slip the skins off under cold, running water. Slice into wedges that are ½ inch thick on the outside edge, cutting along the pit as necessary to free the slice; also cut away and discard any damaged areas. Cut enough slices to fill the pint jar completely, plus a few extra (the slices pack more tightly when they've been cooked for a bit).

In non-aluminum saucepan, combine sugar, vinegar, water, cloves and cinnamon stick. Heat to boiling over medium-high heat, then cook, stirring constantly, until sugar dissolves. Add peach slices; adjust heat so mixture is simmering and cook until peaches are tender but not mushy, 5 to 10 minutes. Use a slotted spoon to transfer the peaches to the prepared jar; also slip the cinnamon stick and cloves into the jar. Pour the vinegar mixture over the peaches, filling to ½ inch from the top; discard excess vinegar mixture. Seal jar and set aside until cool. Refrigerate for at least a week to allow flavors to blend before serving; keep refrigerated.

You could also can the peaches, especially if you're preparing more than one pint. If you'll be canning the peaches, cook them a bit less, so they're just barely tender; they will get additional cooking during the canning process. Process in a hot-water bath for 10 minutes (see pg. 185).

PEARS *(Pyrus communis* and others*)*

Wild pears are found occasionally in our area, as remnants of old orchards or homestead gardens. Some were planted by American Indians as they moved westward; still others have been "planted" by birds, or by humans discarding a pear core into the woods. Regardless of their origins, wild pears are typically much smaller than their domestic cousins, sometimes only an inch across (although often larger, occasionally up to 4 inches in length). Generally, they have only a slight neck, and often, they have no perceptible neck at all, appearing rounded or slightly lumpy. Depending on the original variety, they may develop a reddish blush when ripe, but many are green, yellowish or greenish-yellow when ripe. Pears are ripe when the flesh is no longer hard; like commercial pears, wild pears will soften more if they are allowed to sit at room temperature for a day or two.

Most wild pears are fairly small, sometimes weighing only an ounce or two. Compare that to a domestic pear that tips the scales at 8 to 12 ounces, and you can see that it takes a lot of wild pears to amount to much!

Because wild pears are so much smaller than commercially grown pears, they don't work well for recipes that call for whole, halved or quartered pears. However, chopped wild pears can be used in recipes calling for chopped commercial pears. It may take a lot of wild pears to prepare those recipes, though; the smallest wild pears weigh an ounce or perhaps two. If you've got a mix of ripe and unripe wild pears, refrigerate the ripe ones until the others have ripened, then combine the two batches to prepare your recipe. A few underripe pears, cooked with ripe pears, add pectin to the mix.

Wild pears can be dehydrated, either in slices or quarters; prepare them as directed for crabapples in the instructions on pgs. 182–184. If you want to try making pear juice to prepare jelly, follow the directions for crabapple juice on pg. 6.

Callery pears (*Pyrus calleryana*) have been widely planted as ornamental trees. The fruits are round, about ½ inch across, with speckled, bronze-colored skins; they are produced in great quantity on the trees, growing upright on the stems and looking somewhat like bronze crabapples. The original cultivar, 'Bradford,' was bred to produce sterile fruits that wouldn't create nuisance saplings. However, the trees were found to be susceptible to breakage from snow and wind, so cultivars with stronger branches were bred. The new cultivars have viable seeds, and the trees have escaped into the wild, invading disturbed areas and other locations where they are sometimes considered a nuisance. Fruits remain fairly hard until late in the season, and most people consider them ornamental rather than edible because they are so small and hard. However, they can be eaten; they are hard most of the season, but have a definite pear flavor. I've never cooked with them, but I would treat them the same as small crabapples (pg. 6).

Crisp Pear Tart

This gorgeous tart tastes as good as it looks. Serve it for a special occasion.

½ cup ricotta cheese

Prepared pastry for single-crust pie

**3½ cups quartered wild pears (about 1¼ pounds),
peeled, quartered and cored before measuring**

3 tablespoons (packed) brown sugar

A pinch of salt

2 tablespoons unsalted butter

¼ cup ground almonds (1 ounce)

Place ricotta in a wire-mesh strainer set over a bowl; refrigerate while you prepare the pears. Heat oven to 375°F. Fit pastry into a 9-inch quiche pan; fold excess pastry over inside the pan as necessary, then press together to make a thicker edge. Blind-bake pastry to lightly golden (see "Blind Baking Pie Crusts" on pg. 61). Remove pan from oven and set aside to cool; it can sit at room temperature for several hours before final assembly.

Meanwhile, in mixing bowl, combine pears, brown sugar and salt, stirring to coat. Melt butter in large, heavy-bottomed skillet over medium heat. Add pear mixture. Cook, gently stirring occasionally, until juices have been re-absorbed and pears are browning in spots; this will take 20 to 25 minutes. Remove from heat and set aside. The pears can sit at room temperature for up to an hour before final assembly of the tart; for longer storage, refrigerate the pears, then warm to room temperature before using (the ricotta can be allowed to drain for several hours).

When you're ready for final baking, place oven rack 6 inches from broiler element; heat broiler. Spread drained ricotta evenly in bottom of pre-baked tart crust (discard the liquid that has dripped out); sprinkle almonds evenly over ricotta. Cover edges of crust with strips of foil; this prevents over-browning during the final cooking. Spoon pears over almonds, distributing evenly. Place tart under broiler for 3 to 6 minutes, until the pears develop a few brown spots; be careful that the pears don't burn. Remove foil strips; serve immediately.

The pears are cooked separately from the crust; just before serving, the pears are added to the crust and the whole thing is finished off for a few minutes under the broiler. As a result, the crust remains crisp and flaky, and the filling is flavorful and tender without being mushy.

Pear Filling

About ½ cup; easily increased

1 cup cored, chopped pears

1½ tablespoons lemon juice

2 teaspoons water

1½ tablespoons (packed) brown sugar

A pinch of nutmeg

In small, heavy-bottomed non-aluminum saucepan, combine pears, lemon juice and water. Cook over medium heat, stirring frequently, until pears are tender and mixture has thickened, about 10 minutes. Stir in brown sugar and nutmeg; cook for about a minute longer to dissolve sugar. Cool before using.

Use this to prepare Easy Bear Claws (pg. 30), Fruit-Striped Cookie Fingers (pg. 145), or Fruit-Filled Muffins (pg. 163). Refrigerate extra filling, and use it to top oatmeal or toast.

Pear Butter

Variable quantity; make as much as you wish

This rich, dark spread has a wonderful pear flavor. Use it on toast, or spread over pancakes.

Wild pears

Water

Sugar

Optional: Cinnamon, nutmeg, pie spice (any or all, as you prefer)

Cut the pears into quarters, then remove and discard the stems and blossom remnants; add pears to a heavy-bottomed non-aluminum saucepan. (Don't try to make pear butter from fewer than a quart of wild pears; the amount of the cooking purée will be so small that it will burn.) Add cold water to not quite cover the pear pieces. Heat to boiling over medium-high heat, and boil until the fruit is tender, 10 to 15 minutes. Cool slightly, then strain through a food mill or conical strainer. Discard skins and seeds from food mill.

Proceed as directed for Plum Butter, pg. 134.

Variation: Substitute wild apples for the wild pears, or prepare the butter with a mix of the two fruits.

See companion *Wild Berries & Fruits Field Guide of IN, KY and OH* – page 52   **123**

Smoked Pork Chops with Pears and Mustard

2 servings

Mustard and apple cider combine with the pears to make a delicious sauce for smoked pork chops. This dish is perfect for fall, when wild pears are at their full ripeness. Serve with wild rice, or a wild rice blend.

1 tablespoon unsalted butter

2 smoked pork chops (6 to 8 ounces each)

8 ounces quartered, skin-on wild pears (about 1½ cups), quartered and cored before measuring

¼ cup diced onion

1 teaspoon mustard seeds

¾ cup apple cider

1 tablespoon Dijon mustard

In large skillet, melt butter over medium-high heat. Add pork chops and brown on both sides. Transfer chops to a plate; set aside. Add pears, onion and mustard seed to skillet. Cook over medium-high heat, stirring frequently, for 5 minutes, until pears begin to brown in spots. In measuring cup, combine apple cider and Dijon mustard, stirring to blend. Pour into skillet, stirring to loosen browned bits and to combine liquid with pear mixture. Return pork chops to skillet, laying them on top of the pears. Reduce heat to medium and cook for 10 minutes, shaking pan occasionally to prevent sticking and turning chops once. Serve chops with pears and pan sauce.

The pears can be peeled before using, if you prefer. Personally, I like the texture of the peels in this dish, but it will work just fine either way.

Other recipes in this book using wild pears:
Pear and Chokeberry Mincemeat, pg. 48
Wild Berry or Fruit Leather, pg. 184
As a substitute in Hawthorn and Sausage Brunch Casserole, pg. 83

Quick ideas for using wild pears:
Cut a few up and add them to the mix when preparing apple pie.

PERSIMMONS *(Diospyros virginiana)*

Wild persimmons are a late-ripening fruit, often found hanging on leafless branches into early winter. When properly ripe, a persimmon is so soft that it is like a skin full of jelly; inexperienced foragers may think the fruit spoiled because it is darkened and wrinkled. However, any forager who samples an underripe persimmon will quickly learn to wait until the fruit is jelly-soft; underripe persimmons are extremely astringent and unpleasant to eat, or even to taste. Ripe persimmons, however, have a rich, sweet flavor; in fact, wild persimmons are much more flavorful than the domestic varieties found in supermarkets during fall and winter.

Old-time country lore says the weather can be predicted by looking at the shape inside a split-open persimmon seed. A spoon indicates a snowy winter; if a knife is seen, the winter will be cold and icy, while a fork predicts a mild winter.

Experienced foragers look for ripe persimmons that have fallen from the tree, hoping to find some that have landed, intact, on a cushion of leaves. Slightly underripe persimmons may be collected and placed on the countertop until jelly-soft, but the flavor will not be as full as tree-ripened fruits.

Interestingly, underripe persimmons can be dehydrated successfully; the astringency disappears, and the dehydrated fruit is delightfully sweet and chewy. (See pgs. 182–184 for instructions.) If dehydrating underripe persimmons, choose fruits that are orange and just starting to soften. Purée made from ripe persimmons makes an outstanding fruit leather (pg. 184).

When looking for recipes using persimmons, don't be fooled by those calling for sliced persimmons; these were written for Fuyu persimmons, a domesticated, non-astringent variety that can be eaten when still as firm as an apple. Recipes written for Hachiya, another domesticated variety, are a better choice; like wild persimmons, Hachiya are astringent, and must be jelly-soft before eating. (If you see persimmons in the store, the Fuyu are flattened, while Hachiya are acorn-shaped with a soft point at the bottom.)

To prepare wild persimmons, pull off (or cut away) and discard the dried floral remnants (calyx) at the top of each fruit. **For chunky pulp** (which can be mashed or chopped), cut fruits in half and use a teaspoon to scoop the flesh into a mixing bowl, scraping off and then discarding the skins. Pick through the pulp and remove any seeds; most wild persimmons have several flat, brown seeds, but some are seedless. Scrape the pulp off the seeds as best you can; they're very slippery! A dozen average wild persimmons will yield about 1 cup of chunky pulp. **For smooth purée,** cut fruits in half and process them (skins still on) through a food mill or potato ricer; it will separate the skin and seeds, which can be discarded. You should get about 1 cup of purée from each quart of fruit.

Persimmon pulp or purée can be frozen in freezer-safe, airtight containers; it may darken when thawed, but the flavor will still be fine. You can also can the pulp or purée in a water-bath canner; process half-pints for 30 minutes (see pg. 185 for information about canning). Some people like to freeze whole persimmons, and eat the frozen fruit right out of the skin; the frozen flesh is somewhat like sherbet.

Persimmon-Pistachio Snack Cake

15 servings

Sturdy enough to eat out of hand during coffee break, yet still moist and delicious, these spicy squares will make you a hero at the office. They also make a great after-school snack.

1 cup persimmon purée or mashed persimmon

1 teaspoon baking soda

1 egg

½ cup vegetable oil

1 cup sugar

1 teaspoon Chinese five-spice powder, or 1½ teaspoons pie spice

½ teaspoon salt

1¾ cups all-purpose flour

¾ cup chopped pistachios (3 ounces)

Glaze:

¾ cup confectioners' sugar

1½ tablespoons fresh orange juice

¼ teaspoon vanilla extract

Heat oven to 350°F. In small bowl, stir together persimmon and baking soda; set aside. Grease and flour a 13x9-inch baking dish; set aside.

In large mixing bowl, whisk together the egg and oil until smooth. Add sugar, five-spice powder and salt; whisk again. Check the persimmon pulp; it should have set up and become firm (if not, let it stand for another few minutes, until it has set). Scoop the firm persimmon pulp into the egg mixture, then use the whisk to break it up; whisk everything together until smooth. Add flour; stir with a wooden spoon until just mixed. Finally, stir in the nuts. Scrape into prepared pan, spreading evenly; smooth the top with a table knife. Bake until a toothpick inserted into the center comes out clean, about 30 minutes. Transfer dish to a wire rack and allow to cool completely.

When cake is completely cool, stir together all glaze ingredients in a small bowl. Spread evenly over the cake. Cut into squares. The cake will keep, tightly covered with foil, for a day or two; refrigerate or freeze for longer storage.

Persimmon Frozen Yogurt

Pale orange, creamy and delicious, this has a tangy sweetness that is very refreshing.

1⅓ cups plain yogurt, regular or reduced-fat (not fat-free)

¾ cup smooth persimmon purée

1 tablespoon light corn syrup

1 tablespoon freshly squeezed orange juice

½ cup sugar

⅓ cup whole milk

1 teaspoon unflavored gelatin

Prepare ice cream freezer as directed by manufacturer. In medium mixing bowl, stir together the yogurt, persimmon purée, corn syrup and orange juice; cover with plastic wrap and refrigerate until needed. In small saucepan, combine sugar and milk. Heat over low heat, stirring constantly, until sugar dissolves and mixture no longer looks grainy, 2 to 3 minutes. Remove from heat; set aside until just warm, about 5 minutes.

When the milk mixture has cooled to about 100°F, sprinkle gelatin over the top; let stand for about a minute, then stir continuously for a minute longer. Pour mixture into bowl with persimmon, and stir all together very well. Re-cover and refrigerate for at least an hour, and as long as 2 hours.

When mixture has chilled for 1 to 2 hours, transfer to prepared ice-cream maker and churn until mixture holds a soft shape, generally 15 to 20 minutes. Scoop into plastic container, cover tightly and freeze for at least 2 hours before serving. The frozen yogurt will keep in the freezer for a week or so; if it becomes too hard to scoop, place container in the refrigerator for about 30 minutes to soften the frozen yogurt slightly before serving.

Variation: Add ½ cup toffee bits (found in the baking aisle with the chocolate chips) to the mixture during the last 5 minutes of churning. The toffee is a nice complement to the persimmon flavor, and the texture is a pleasant addition.

Persimmon-Glazed Stuffed Chicken
4 servings

This delicious restaurant-style dish is one of my favorite recipes in this book. Serve it at a special dinner party; it's especially good for guests who have never tried wild persimmons.

4 bone-in chicken breast halves (9 to 10 ounces each)

3 ounces Brie or other soft, ripened cheese

2 teaspoons crumbled dried sage

Salt and freshly ground pepper

²/₃ cup mashed persimmon

3 tablespoons extra virgin olive oil

2 cloves garlic, minced or crushed

1 tablespoon apple cider vinegar

1 tablespoon honey

Heat oven to 400°F. Remove and discard skin from chicken breast halves. With a sharp paring or boning knife, cut a deep pocket in each breast half from the thickest side, cutting almost to the thin side. Cut Brie into 4 equal slices; roll in dried sage. Stuff one sage-encrusted piece of Brie into each pocket, working the cheese deeply into the pocket so the edge of the chicken breast seals around and over the cheese. Score the top of the chicken breasts (on the side where the skin was) with shallow slits about 1 inch apart. Sprinkle with salt and pepper. Place stuffed breasts into a 13x9-inch baking dish with the thick sides facing the outside edges of the pan; set aside.

In small mixing bowl, combine mashed persimmon, olive oil, garlic, vinegar and honey; stir well. Pour over chicken breasts, rubbing into slits; turn breasts to coat back side, then turn so the slit side is facing up again. Bake for 40 minutes, or until internal temperature of chicken reads 165°F. Remove dish from oven; cover loosely and let stand for 5 to 10 minutes before serving. Scoop any drippings from baking dish into a small serving bowl, and serve with chicken.

Chicken on the Bone
Chicken breast halves can be very dry if overcooked. Pieces that still have the bone attached will be more juicy when cooked, even if the skin has been removed. Be sure to let your guests know that the chicken still has the bone—and cartilage—attached, so they know to avoid these inedible parts.

Persimmon Jam

Slather some of this delicious jam on hot, buttered whole wheat toast for a perfect breakfast.

Ripe persimmons (1 heaping quart of whole persimmons will yield about 1 cup of finished jam)

2 tablespoons sugar for each cup of cleaned persimmon

½ teaspoon freshly squeezed lemon juice for each cup of cleaned persimmon

Pull off (or cut away) and discard the dried floral remnants (calyx) at the top of each fruit. Cut fruits in half and use a teaspoon to scoop the flesh into a mixing bowl, scraping off and then discarding the skins. Pick through the pulp and remove any seeds and any discolored portions. Measure the cleaned persimmon flesh and transfer to a heavy-bottomed saucepan. For each cup of cleaned persimmon, add 2 tablespoons sugar. Heat over medium heat until simmering, breaking up larger chunks with your spoon. Cook at a strong simmer or slow boil, stirring almost constantly, for about 10 minutes, or until jam has thickened and will hold a soft shape when a bit is placed on a plate. Remove from heat; stir in ½ teaspoon lemon juice for each cup of cleaned persimmon you started with. Transfer to clean jars and refrigerate for up to 3 weeks, or freeze for longer storage. You may also can half-pints in a water-bath canner for 10 minutes, following the general instructions on pg. 185.

Persimmon Filling

½ cup mashed persimmon

1 tablespoon (packed) brown sugar

½ teaspoon freshly squeezed lemon juice

In small, heavy-bottomed non-aluminum saucepan, combine persimmon, brown sugar and lemon juice. Cook over medium heat, stirring constantly, until the sugar dissolves and mixture thickens slightly, about 5 minutes. Cool before using.

Use this to prepare Easy Bear Claws (pg. 30), Fruit-Striped Cookie Fingers (pg. 145), or Fruit-Filled Muffins (pg. 163). Refrigerate extra filling, and use it to top oatmeal or toast.

Persimmon Quick Bread

1 loaf (10 to 12 servings)

Rich and moist, with a subtle flavor from the spices.

1 cup persimmon purée or mashed persimmon

1 teaspoon baking soda

1½ cups all-purpose flour

¾ cup sugar

1 teaspoon cinnamon

½ teaspoon ground cardamom

½ teaspoon salt

2 eggs

½ cup vegetable oil

½ cup chopped pecans, hickory nuts or other nuts

½ cup dried cranberries (craisins)

Heat oven to 350°F. In small bowl, stir together persimmon and baking soda; set aside. Spray a standard-sized loaf pan with nonstick spray; set aside.

Set a wire-mesh strainer over a large mixing bowl. Add flour, sugar, cinnamon, cardamom and salt; shake to sift into bowl. In a separate medium mixing bowl, whisk together eggs and oil until smooth. Check the persimmon pulp; it should have set up and become firm (if not, let it stand for another few minutes, until it has set). Scoop the firm persimmon pulp into the egg mixture, then use the whisk to break it up; whisk everything together until smooth. Scrape the persimmon mixture into the bowl with the flour, then stir together with a wooden spoon until just mixed. Add pecans and cranberries; stir until mixed in. Scrape into prepared loaf pan. Bake until a toothpick inserted into the center comes out clean, about 1¼ hours. Place pan on wire rack to cool for about 15 minutes, then run a knife around the edges and turn the loaf out onto the rack to cool completely.

Persimmon and Baking Soda

Persimmons have a high tannin content; that's what makes them "puckery" when they're underripe. Alkaline ingredients such as baking soda neutralize the tannins, and cause the persimmon pulp to set up into a firm mass filled with tiny carbon dioxide bubbles. The trapped CO_2 bubbles produce moist, tender baked goods.

Persimmon Smoothie

A quick and healthy breakfast with a subtly tropical flavor.

1 cup soy milk, rice milk or regular milk

½ cup plain yogurt (regular, low-fat or fat-free)

⅓ to ½ cup mashed persimmon or seedless persimmon pieces

2 teaspoons honey or other sweetener of choice

Half of a banana

½ cup ice cubes

In blender, combine milk, yogurt, persimmon, honey and banana. Pulse on-and-off on high a few times, then blend on high for about 15 seconds, or until smooth. Add ice cubes; blend until frothy, about 5 seconds. Serve immediately.

Variation: Substitute ½ cup of any bramble (raspberries, blackberries or dewberries), soft-seeded berry (blueberries, huckleberries or serviceberries), or soft fruit such as mashed pawpaw or strawberries for the persimmon. Adjust honey as needed, depending on the sweetness of the fruit.

Other recipes in this book featuring persimmons:
Dehydrating Wild Berries and Fruits, pg. 182–184
Wild Berry or Fruit Leather, pg. 184
As a substitute in Apple Donut Holes, pg. 10
As a substitute in Autumn Olive "Berries" for Baking, pg. 14

See companion *Wild Berries & Fruits Field Guide of IN, KY and OH* – page 80   **131**

PLUMS: AMERICAN WILD PLUM, GOOSE PLUMS and MEXICAN PLUM
(Prunus americana, P. hortulana, P. munsoniana and P. mexicana)

Wild plums are easy to identify; they look a lot like the ones you buy in the store, but smaller. Ripe American wild plums are typically bright reddish-orange; ripe goose plums are red or yellow, while Mexican plums are purplish-red. Eating quality of all wild plums varies between species and also from tree to tree; some are too tart to eat raw and are best used for cooked dishes. Others are sweet and juicy, begging to be popped into the mouth and savored on the spot.

Note that plums don't ripen well off the tree, so it's best to harvest only ripe plums, which will be slightly soft. Unripe plums can cause digestive upset.

Plums can be cut from the pit for use in recipes; they are also used to make purée or, less commonly, juice. Unlike many wild fruits, cut-up plums work well in savory dishes as well as sweet ones. I've never encountered a wild plum whose flesh separated easily and cleanly from the pit; unlike some domestic plums, wild plums cling tightly to the pit. Use a paring knife to cut the flesh away, cutting as close to the pit as you can. Plum skin is a bit sour, but I generally leave the skin on the fruit when I'm pitting. If you wish to remove the skins, drop a few whole plums into a pan of boiling water, then boil until the skin splits slightly; this takes about a minute. Immediately transfer the plums to a bowl filled with ice water. You can now peel the skins off, then cut the flesh away from the pit and proceed with your recipe.

To prepare purée or juice, it's not necessary to remove the pits; simply cut the plums into rough halves, cutting alongside the pit, and place in a non-aluminum saucepan or pot. For purée, add enough water to come about one-quarter of the way up the plums; for juice, add enough to come about halfway up. Heat to boiling over high heat, then reduce heat and simmer, stirring occasionally, for 10 minutes, or until the plums are very soft.* **For purée,** transfer the cooked fruit mixture to a food mill and process until the pits are largely scraped clean; remove pits individually, then process the mixture remaining in the food mill until all that's left in the food mill is skins. **For juice,** transfer the cooked fruit mixture to a strainer lined with doubled, dampened cheesecloth and let it drip for 30 minutes; if you're making jelly, don't squeeze the fruit or the jelly will be cloudy. After the clear liquid has dripped away, set it aside and squeeze the fruit into a different container; you can use this slightly cloudy juice as a beverage or for cooking.

Yield varies quite a bit with plums; some are very fleshy and produce a good quantity of cut-up fruit or purée, while others are thin-fleshed, yielding much less. If you've found nicely fleshy wild plums, you'll probably get a cup of cut-up chunks (uncooked) per dozen fruits; a pound of fleshy plums typically produces ½ to ¾ cup of cooked purée, or 1½ cups of juice.

*Don't crush the pits during cooking or straining. Plum pits contain small amounts of a cyanide-forming compound that can cause illness if eaten in large quantities.

Plum-Dandy Oatmeal Squares

These tasty squares hold up well in a lunchbox.

1½ cups cut-up wild plums, pitted and cut into ½-inch chunks before measuring

3 tablespoons apple juice, other juice or water

1 tablespoon honey

1½ cups all-purpose flour

½ cup old-fashioned rolled oats

1½ cups (packed) golden brown sugar

¼ teaspoon baking soda

A pinch of salt

⅓ cup vegetable oil

3 tablespoons frozen orange juice concentrate

2 tablespoons cold butter, cut into several chunks

In small saucepan, combine plums, apple juice and honey. Heat to boiling over medium-high heat, then reduce heat so mixture is simmering. Cook, stirring frequently, until plums break up and mixture thickens, about 10 minutes. Remove from heat; set aside until cool.

Heat oven to 350°F. Spray 8-inch-square baking dish with nonstick spray; set aside. In mixing bowl, combine flour, rolled oats, brown sugar, baking soda and salt; mix well with a wooden spoon. Remove ½ cup of the flour mixture, transferring to a small bowl; set aside. Add oil and orange juice concentrate to flour remaining in mixing bowl; stir with wooden spoon until well-mixed and crumbly. Pat flour mixture into prepared baking dish, pressing firmly. Spoon cooled plum filling over crust, spreading evenly; set aside.

Add cold butter to the ½ cup flour mixture in the small bowl. Rub together with your fingertips until the mixture is crumbly. Sprinkle topping over plum filling. Bake until golden brown, about 30 minutes. Cool on wire rack before cutting into squares.

Plum Butter

Plum butter is easy to make in almost any quantity, because it needs no added pectin (and therefore does not require precise measurements). It's fabulous as a spread for toast, or used to top pancakes, waffles or hot cereal.

Wild plums

Water

Sugar

Optional: Cinnamon, cardamom, nutmeg (any or all, as you prefer)

Cut the flesh away from the pits, adding them to a saucepan as you go. (Don't try to make plum butter with fewer than 12 plums; the amount of the cooking purée will be so small that it will burn.) Add cold water to cover the plum pieces. Heat to boiling over medium-high heat, and boil until skins are tender, about 10 minutes. Cool slightly, then strain through a food mill or conical strainer; you could also strain the plums through a wire-mesh strainer, stirring and pushing the fruit through with a wooden spoon.

Measure the strained pulp and transfer to a heavy-bottomed non-aluminum saucepan. Sterilize enough half-pint canning jars, bands and new lids (see pg. 185) to hold the finished plum butter (as a guideline, you'd need 4 half-pint jars for 3 cups of strained pulp). Heat to boiling over medium-high heat, then add ½ to ⅞ cup of sugar per cup of strained plums (the amount depends on the sweetness of the plums and your personal preference), stirring until the sugar dissolves. If using spices, add them now; try ¼ teaspoon of cinnamon or cardamom (or both) per cup of strained pulp, and/or a healthy pinch of nutmeg. Adjust heat so the mixture is boiling, but not so vigorously that the bubbles explode. Cook, stirring frequently, until the mixture is very thick; this will take 15 to 30 minutes, depending on how runny the strained pulp was. Transfer to prepared canning jars. Process in a water-bath canner for 10 minutes, or refrigerate.

Wild Plum Jelly

2¾ cups wild plum juice

Half of a 1.75-ounce box powdered pectin

½ teaspoon butter, optional (helps reduce foaming)

3¼ cups sugar

Prepare and process as directed in Jelly Instructions (using pectin), pg. 178.

Asian-Inspired Plum Sauce

About 1¼ cups

This lovely, jewel-like sauce packs a punch from the hot pepper and gingerroot.

2 cloves garlic

1-inch chunk of peeled fresh gingerroot

1 small hot red pepper, seeds and stem removed

Half of a small white onion, cut into 1-inch pieces

Half of a red bell pepper, cored and cut into 1-inch chunks

**2 cups cut-up wild plums, pitted and cut into
½-inch chunks before measuring**

⅓ cup brown sugar

⅓ cup seasoned rice vinegar

¼ cup orange juice

½ teaspoon ground coriander

½ teaspoon salt

In food processor, chop garlic, gingerroot and hot pepper until very fine. Add onion and bell pepper; pulse a few times to chop. Add plums; pulse until everything is chopped to medium texture. Transfer mixture to medium, heavy-bottomed non-aluminum sauce-pan; add remaining ingredients. Heat to boiling over medium-high heat; reduce heat and simmer, stirring frequently, until thick, about 30 minutes. Transfer to clean jars; cool completely. Store in refrigerator.

Serve this with egg rolls or chicken wings, or add it to stir-fries. It's also great when brushed over ribs, pork chops or chicken just before taking them from the grill.

Ham Slice with Piquant Plum Sauce

A savory plum sauce adds a sweet-and-tangy note to ham in this easy weeknight supper.

¼ cup minced shallots

1 tablespoon butter

**1½ cups cut-up wild plums, pitted and cut into
½- to ¾-inch chunks before measuring**

⅓ cup dry sherry

2 tablespoons maple syrup

1 tablespoon coarse (prepared) mustard

¼ teaspoon chili powder blend

1 bone-in ham slice, about 1¼ pounds

Heat oven to 400°F. In saucepan, cook shallots in butter over medium heat, stirring frequently, for 5 minutes. Add plums; cook, stirring frequently, for 5 minutes. Add sherry, maple syrup, mustard and chili powder; stir well. Cook, stirring occasionally, for about 5 minutes, or until plums have softened but still retain their shape. Remove from heat.

Place ham in a baking dish large enough to hold it. Spoon about ⅓ cup of the plum sauce over the ham, spreading evenly. Bake for 10 minutes, or until ham is hot all the way through and sauce is starting to glaze. If you like, turn the broiler on and broil for a minute or so to caramelize the glaze. Cut ham into 4 portions; serve with remaining sauce.

Variation: This recipe would also work with smoked pork chops.

Plum Filling

This filling is really pretty, and adds wonderful jewel tones to baked goods.

1 cup cut-up wild plums, pitted and cut into ¼-inch chunks before measuring

2 tablespoons sugar

1 tablespoon grated apple

1 teaspoon lemon juice

In small, heavy-bottomed saucepan, combine all ingredients. Crush fruit gently with a potato masher to start juices flowing. Heat to boiling over medium-high heat. Reduce heat; cover and simmer, stirring occasionally, until fruit is tender, 5 to 8 minutes. Mash again. Increase heat to medium-high, and boil, stirring frequently, until thick, about 5 minutes. Cool before using.

Use this to prepare Easy Bear Claws (pg. 30), Fruit-Striped Cookie Fingers (pg. 145), or Fruit-Filled Muffins (pg. 163). Refrigerate extra filling, and use to top oatmeal or toast.

Other recipes in this book featuring wild plums:
Spicy Plum Chutney, pg. 160
Six Recipes Using Wild Fruit Juice or Syrup, pgs. 172–176
Wild Berry or Fruit Syrup, pg. 177
Dehydrating Wild Berries and Fruits, pgs. 182–184

Quick ideas for using wild plums:
Use cut-up wild plums in any recipe that calls for domestic plums; you may need to increase the sugar slightly if your plums are tart.

Sweeten plum purée to taste, then use it to make a delicious fruit leather (see pg. 184 for information on making leathers).

Plum juice makes a wonderful breakfast drink when sweetened to taste. If you're making juice to drink rather than to make jelly, don't worry about making clear juice; squeeze the cheesecloth-wrapped fruit to get more juice. The juice will be thicker than that used to make jelly, and the extra body is nice in juice for drinking.

PRICKLY PEARS *(Opuntia* spp.*)*

Prickly pears are typically found in dry, sandy or rocky areas. They're easy to recognize; look for flat, spiny cactus pads with reddish egg-shaped or oblong fruits on top. Don't attempt to pick the fruits unless you're wearing thick leather gloves, though; in addition to the stout spines you may see, both pads and fruits are armed with hairlike, virtually invisible spines that break off and lodge in your skin at the slightest touch. Even if a plant has few or no stout spines, you can be assured that the hairlike spines are present. The best way to deal with the invisible spines is to singe them off. Use a tongs to rotate the fruit over a gas flame (stovetop, camping stove, torch or side burner on a gas grill); the fine spines burn off instantly.

The pads of the prickly pear cactus are a traditional Mexican vegetable, referred to as nopales or nopalitos.

To peel the singed fruit, cut the ends off, then make a lengthwise slit through the skin and peel the skin off. If the fruit is very small and too difficult to peel, slit it open and scrape the flesh out with a teaspoon. Some sources say that you can run the entire fruit—skin and all—through a food mill, but I prefer not to take a chance that a spine is still embedded in the skin; I'd rather not find out what it's like to swallow one!

The seeds are about ⅛ inch across and extremely hard, and most people—including me—prefer to avoid eating them. But if you're confident of your dental work and like a challenge, you can eat the flesh with the seeds intact; they won't make you sick.

For purée, process the peeled fruits, raw or cooked as described below, through a food mill. Eight ounces of uncooked fruit (weighed after peeling) will yield about ½ cup of smooth purée. As an option, place the peeled fruits in a microwave-safe bowl with a little water; cover and microwave at 50% power until the fruit is soft (timing varies depending on quantity, but it's usually just a few minutes). The fruits can be processed in the food mill, or poured into a wire-mesh strainer and stirred vigorously with a spoon to press the softened flesh through the mesh. Yield will be a bit higher with the microwave method, but the purée will be thinner than with the uncooked method. With either method, I scrape the seedy pulp from the food mill afterward and simmer it for 10 minutes with enough water to barely cover it; I strain that through my wire-mesh strainer to get a thin juice, which I add to juice prepared from whole fruits using one of the methods below.

To prepare **uncooked juice**, process peeled fruits in a blender with a small amount of water until the fruit is puréed. Pour everything into a wire-mesh strainer that is set over a large bowl, and let the juice drip into the bowl; stir it vigorously with a wooden spoon to extract as much liquid as possible, then discard the seedy pulp. Eight ounces of fruit (weighed after peeling) will yield about 1 cup of medium-body, slightly cloudy juice. For **cooked juice,** cut the peeled fruits into halves or quarters and place in a saucepan with water to barely cover. Simmer for about 10 minutes, mashing once or twice with a potato masher, then strain through doubled cheesecloth; squeeze the cheesecloth well at the end, then discard the cheesecloth and its contents. This method yields about 1½ cups of clear, thin juice from 8 ounces of peeled fruits.

Prickly Pear Vinaigrette

This vivid-red dressing is absolutely outstanding on a salad of tender greens that is topped with some crumbled blue cheese and a few chopped walnuts.

½ cup seasoned rice vinegar

½ teaspoon mixed pickling spice

3 ounces peeled prickly pear, cut into ¼-inch slices

⅓ cup extra virgin olive oil

1 teaspoon Dijon mustard

½ teaspoon mixed dried herb blend

1 small garlic clove, pressed or finely minced

Salt and freshly ground pepper to taste

In small, non-aluminum saucepan, combine vinegar and pickling spice. Heat to boiling over high heat; remove from heat and let steep for 10 minutes. Return to stove, and heat just to boiling over medium-high heat. Add prickly pear slices. Adjust heat so mixture is simmering gently, then cook for 10 minutes, mashing after a few minutes. Let cool slightly, then pour into a small wire-mesh strainer set over a 2-cup measure. Let drip for 5 minutes; discard fruit pulp and spices from the strainer. Set liquid aside until completely cool.

In a clean pint jar, combine cooled liquid with olive oil, mustard, herbs and garlic; cover tightly and shake very well to blend. Taste, and add salt and pepper to your preference. Store in the refrigerator in a tightly capped jar; it will keep for several months. Before using, shake well to blend.

Chocolate-Prickly Pear Fudge   32 pieces

Prickly pear and chocolate pair nicely together in this rich, dark fudge.

1½ cups white sugar

½ cup (packed) dark brown sugar

½ cup prickly pear purée

½ cup heavy cream

2 tablespoons light corn syrup

⅛ teaspoon salt

2 ounces unsweetened baking chocolate

3 tablespoons butter, plus additional for greasing pan

½ teaspoon vanilla extract

½ cup chopped walnuts or other nuts, optional

In a heavy-bottomed, deep saucepan or pot, combine white and brown sugars, prickly pear purée, cream, corn syrup, salt and chocolate. Cook over medium heat, stirring constantly with a wooden spoon, until chocolate melts and sugars dissolve; mixture will no longer look cloudy. Continue cooking, stirring almost constantly, until mixture reaches 236°F (soft-ball stage; see "Fudge Tips," below); adjust heat as necessary so mixture boils fairly vigorously but does not foam up out of the saucepan. Remove from heat; drop the 3 tablespoons butter, cut into several chunks, into the pot without stirring. Let stand until mixture cools to about 110°F (lukewarm); this will take about 45 minutes. While the mixture cools, butter the inside of a standard-sized loaf pan; set aside until needed.

When mixture has cooled to lukewarm, add vanilla. Stir vigorously with a wooden spoon until mixture loses its glossy sheen and begins to thicken, 7 to 10 minutes. Scrape into the prepared loaf pan; smooth the top with a rubber spatula. Sprinkle with nuts, pressing them gently into the surface with the spatula. Set aside to cool completely, then cut into 32 squares. Store at room temperature in a tightly sealed container for up to a week.

Fudge Tips
- *When heated above boiling, sugar tends to form crystals; the small amount of corn syrup used here helps prevent crystallization.*
- *The fudge is cooked to 236°F, which is referred to as the soft-ball stage. If you don't have a candy thermometer, test the fudge by dropping a small bit of it into a bowl of cold water; when it is at the soft-ball stage, it will form a soft, flexible ball that you can push around with your fingertip.*
- *Watch the fudge mixture as it's boiling; if it starts to rise rapidly and threatens to boil over, quickly remove the pan from the heat.*

Prickly Pear Jelly

2 half-pints

1½ cups prickly pear juice

1 tablespoon lemon juice

One-third of a 1.75-ounce box powdered pectin

¼ teaspoon butter, optional (helps reduce foaming)

1½ cups sugar

Prepare and process as directed in Jelly Instructions (using pectin), pg. 178.

Prickly Margarita

2 servings

Here's a wild twist on a classic cocktail . . . colorful and delicious.

¾ cup prickly pear juice

⅓ cup tequila

¼ cup frozen limeade concentrate, thawed enough to measure

2 tablespoons triple sec liqueur

1 tablespoon sugar, or to taste

¾ cup crushed ice

Optional: lime wedge and bar salt for rim of glass

If you like salty Margaritas, run the lime wedge around the edges of two margarita glasses, then dip in salt; set aside. To prepare the Margarita, combine prickly pear juice, tequila, limeade concentrate, triple sec and sugar in blender; pulse several times to blend. Taste, and adjust sweetness to taste if necessary. Add crushed ice to blender; pulse several times, then pour into Margarita glasses and serve immediately.

Other recipes in this book featuring prickly pears:
Six Recipes Using Wild Fruit Juice or Syrup, pgs. 172–176
Wild Berry or Fruit Syrup, pg. 177
Wild Berry or Fruit Leather, pg. 184

Quick ideas for using prickly pears:
For a delightfully different pink lemonade, use half water, half prickly pear juice when mixing up frozen lemonade concentrate.

RASPBERRIES: BLACK, RED and PURPLE-FLOWERING *(Rubus* family)

Two types of raspberry brambles (sprawling vine-like shrubs) grow in our area. Black raspberries (*Rubus occidentalis*) are one of the most delicious wild fruits found in our area; they're easy to identify, abundant and delicious. Red raspberries (*R. idaeus*) are less common in our area, but are a favorite wherever they grow.

The fruits of purple-flowering raspberries are very soft and delicate, and get smashed if layered too deeply in the berry bucket. When picking them to bring home, transport them in flat containers, like those used by delis to hold a half pint of coleslaw.

Purple-flowering raspberries (*R. odoratus*) are also found in our area. Although they're related to the brambles, they grow as waist-high shrubs with large, maple-like leaves. Their fruits are similar to red raspberries, but wider, flatter and more delicate; they can be used in the same way, so are grouped here. Eating quality varies from plant to plant; sample a few before harvesting in any quantity to be sure they are tasty. When picking purple-flowering raspberries, look for fruits that are rich red and soft; pink fruits are underripe and hard, and are usually bitter.

All of the fruits listed here are compound drupes, with lots of small seeds. The seeds are noticeable, but not nearly as bothersome as blackberry seeds; however, some cooks prefer to strain them out when making jam or purée. I seldom bother with this extra step, preferring to enjoy the fruit in its natural state.

To prepare purée or juice, measure the fruit and place in a non-aluminum pot. For purée, add ½ cup water per quart of fruit; for juice, add 1 cup water per quart of fruit. Gently crush the fruit with a potato masher to start the juices flowing. Heat to boiling, then reduce the heat; cover and simmer for about 10 minutes. **For seedless purée,** process the cooked fruit through a food mill, then discard the seeds; if you don't mind the seeds, the purée is ready after cooking. **For juice,** transfer the mixture to a strainer lined with doubled, dampened cheesecloth and let it drip for 30 minutes; if you're making jelly, don't squeeze the fruit or the jelly will be cloudy. After the clear liquid has dripped away, set it aside and squeeze the fruit into a different container; you can use this slightly cloudy juice as a beverage or for cooking, and add the leftover, squeezed fruit to applesauce, pie filling or other cooked fruits. Processed this way, a quart of red raspberries will yield about 1½ cups of purée, or about 2 cups juice; the yield will be slightly less for black raspberries or purple-flowering raspberries.

To avoid cumbersome ingredients lists, most of the recipes on the following pages simply call for raspberries. You may use red or black raspberries for any of them with no adjustments; if you use purple-flowering raspberries, you may wish to increase the sugar slightly, depending on the sweetness of the berries you've picked.

Raspberry Filling

About ½ cup; easily increased

½ teaspoon water

½ teaspoon cornstarch

5 ounces raspberries (about 1 cup)

1 tablespoon grated apple

1 tablespoon sugar

½ teaspoon lemon juice

In small bowl, blend together water and cornstarch; set aside. In small, heavy-bottomed saucepan, combine raspberries, apple, sugar and lemon juice. Crush fruit gently with a potato masher to start juices flowing. Heat to boiling over medium-high heat, then cook, stirring frequently, until mixture is no longer runny; this will take 9 to 11 minutes. Add cornstarch mixture, stirring constantly; cook for 1 to 2 minutes longer, or until thick. Cool before using.

Use this to prepare Easy Bear Claws (pg. 30), Fruit-Striped Cookie Fingers (pg. 145), or Fruit-Filled Muffins (pg. 163). Refrigerate extra filling, and use to top oatmeal or toast.

Raspberry Dip

About 2 cups

This is lovely for a brunch buffet, or as a tea-time snack. Have a pretty jar of toothpicks for the pineapples and pound cake. This recipe also works well with wild strawberries.

16 ounces cream cheese, softened (reduced-fat works fine)

½ cup raspberries (about 2½ ounces)

¼ cup sour cream (reduced-fat works fine)

2 tablespoons honey

1 teaspoon vanilla extract

¼ teaspoon grated orange zest (colored rind only,
with none of the white pith), optional

Dippers for serving (any or all): Pineapple chunks, pound cake cubes,
vanilla wafers, pieces of chocolate bars, or assorted cookies

In food processor, combine all ingredients except dippers; process until smooth. Scrape into serving bowl. Cover and refrigerate for at least 2 hours before serving.

Raspberry Shortcakes

A classic dessert that really shows off the flavor of fresh-picked raspberries.

Shortcakes:

2 cups all-purpose flour, plus additional for rolling dough

3 tablespoons sugar

1 tablespoon baking powder

½ teaspoon salt

½ cup (1 stick) cold unsalted butter, cut into 8 pieces

⅔ cup whole milk, approximate

Filling:

2 cups fresh raspberries (about 10 ounces)

½ cup sugar, or to taste

1 cup whipping cream

½ teaspoon vanilla extract

Prepare the shortcakes: Heat oven to 425°F, and line a baking sheet with kitchen parchment. In food processor, combine 2 cups flour, the sugar, baking powder and salt; pulse a few times to combine. Add cut-up butter; pulse until mixture resembles coarse meal but still has a few pea-sized pieces of butter. With motor running, add milk in a thin stream through the feed tube; use just enough milk so the mixture comes together (don't add too much milk or over-process the dough, or the shortcakes will be tough).

On lightly floured worksurface, knead dough a few times to form a ball; mixture will be sticky at first, but will become less sticky as it picks up flour from the worksurface. Use a rolling pin to roll about ¾ inch thick. Cut 8 circles, using a 3-inch circular cutter (re-roll scraps once if necessary). Transfer to prepared baking sheet. Bake until dough rises and is golden brown, 10 to 15 minutes. Transfer to wire rack while you prepare the filling.

Prepare the filling: Place raspberries in mixing bowl; sprinkle with sugar, tossing gently to coat. Set aside to marinate for a few minutes. In another mixing bowl, beat whipping cream and vanilla with electric mixer until stiff peaks form.

To assemble the shortcakes, use a knife to split each shortcake horizontally. Place one half on an individual dessert plate. Top with about ¼ cup of the raspberries; place second half of shortcake on top. Dollop whipped cream over the top shortcake half; serve immediately.

Fruit-Striped Cookie Fingers

A buttery, rich cookie base is topped with fruit filling in these attractive cookies.

1¾ cups all-purpose flour, plus additional for rolling dough

¼ cup powdered sugar

⅛ teaspoon salt

½ cup (1 stick) cold butter, cut into small pieces

4 ounces cream cheese, cut into 1-inch chunks

1 egg yolk

1 tablespoon orange juice

1 teaspoon vanilla extract

½ cup Raspberry Filling (pg. 143), or other wild fruit filling (see "Filling options" below)

In food processor, combine 1¾ cups flour, the powdered sugar and salt; pulse a few times to mix. Add butter and cream cheese; pulse until mixture is coarse and crumbly. In a small bowl, stir together the egg yolk, orange juice and vanilla. Add to flour mixture; pulse a few times, until mixture just begins to come together (do not over-process, or the cookies will be tough). Transfer dough to a gallon-sized plastic food storage bag. Press with your hands (from the outside of the bag) until dough comes together. Flatten dough into a disk; refrigerate at least 1 hour, or as long as 1 day.

When ready to bake, heat oven to 375°F. Divide dough into 2 parts; refrigerate one while you roll out the other. On lightly floured worksurface, roll dough about ¼ inch thick, keeping the rolled-out dough as square as possible. Trim one edge in a straight line, then use a small ruler to mark 1-inch divisions. Cut the dough into 1-inch-wide strips, cutting on the marks. Lay a chopstick lengthwise in the center of one strip, and press it down into the dough, rolling it back and forth slightly to make a U-shaped channel about ½ inch wide in the center of the strip. Transfer the strip to an ungreased baking sheet. Repeat with remaining strips, keeping them ½ inch apart on the baking sheet. Spoon filling mixture along the channels, mounding it slightly. Bake until golden brown and firm, 23 to 26 minutes. Remove baking sheets from oven, and immediately use a small knife to cut each strip into 1-inch pieces. Transfer to a wire rack to cool completely. Store at room temperature for up to 5 days; refrigerate or freeze for longer storage.

Filling options: This recipe works with any of the following fillings: Apple or Crabapple (pg. 9), Blackberry (pg. 20), Blackhaw (pg. 27), Blueberry (pg. 33), Green Gooseberry (pg. 67), Ground Cherry (pg. 76), Mulberry (pg. 101), Muscadine (pg. 107), Peach (pg. 119), Pear (pg. 123), Persimmon (pg. 129), Plum (pg. 137), Raspberry (pg. 143), Serviceberry (pg. 156), or Strawberry (pg. 161).

Rustic Black Raspberry Tart

5 or 6 servings

This tart is a lovely presentation that is unusual enough to look like a really special treat, but it's super-easy to make. Top with some rich vanilla ice cream for a heavenly dessert.

2½ to 3 cups black raspberries (12 to 15 ounces)

½ cup sugar

3 tablespoons minute tapioca

1 tablespoon lemon juice

Ready-to-use pastry for single-crust pie

2 teaspoons butter, cut into small pieces

Heat oven to 375°F; line a rimmed baking sheet with kitchen parchment. In mixing bowl, combine raspberries, sugar, tapioca and lemon juice; stir gently. Set aside for 15 minutes. After 15 minutes, place pastry on prepared baking sheet. Pile raspberry mixture in the center, staying 1½ inches away from the edges. Working quickly, fold pastry over the edge of the filling, leaving the center exposed; the shape will be irregular, but the filling should be surrounded. Pinch overlapping areas together slightly to seal. Dot exposed filling with butter. Bake until crust is brown and filling is bubbling, 30 to 40 minutes. Let cool slightly before cutting; best served warm, the day it is made.

Ready-to-Use Pie Crust

Many recipes in this book call for "ready-to-use pastry for single- (or double-) crust pie." These days, many cooks choose to purchase ready-made pie crusts from the refrigerator case. These are already rolled out into single-crust form; simply thaw or warm them according to package directions, and use as directed. If you make your own pie crust, roll out the dough (or half the dough at once, if you've made enough for a two-crust pie) on a lightly floured worksurface, and proceed as directed.

Raspberry Jelly

4 half-pints

2¾ cups raspberry juice

Two-thirds of a 1.75-ounce box powdered pectin

½ teaspoon butter, optional (helps reduce foaming)

3⅔ cups sugar

Prepare and process as directed in Jelly Instructions (using pectin), pg. 178.

Raspberry-Balsamic Dressing

About ¾ cup

Serve this with salad made from tender greens; it's especially good if a little feta cheese is added to the salad. You could also drizzle this over cooked, sliced chicken breast that is atop a bed of spinach; garnish with sliced almonds and a few slivers of red onion.

1 cup raspberries (about 5 ounces)

5 tablespoons olive oil

2 tablespoons balsamic vinegar

1 teaspoon Dijon mustard

1 teaspoon honey

½ teaspoon salt

⅛ teaspoon white pepper

1 clove garlic, pressed or very finely minced

Purée raspberries in mini food processor or blender. Scrape into a wire-mesh strainer set over a bowl. Stir with a rubber spatula to press the purée through; discard seeds. Transfer strained purée to a half-pint jar. Add remaining ingredients. Cover tightly and shake well to blend. This will keep in the refrigerator for up to 3 weeks.

Other recipes in this book featuring raspberries:
Refrigerator Cookies with Dried Berries, pg. 15
Wild Berry Vinegar, pg. 19
Fruit Terrine with Elderberry Gel, pg. 62
Rice Pudding with Wild Berries, pg. 103
Fruits of the Forest Pie, pg. 170
Brambleberry Cream Sauce, pg. 171
Six Recipes Using Wild Fruit Juice or Syrup, pgs. 172–176
Wild Berry or Fruit Syrup, pg. 177
Dehydrating Wild Berries and Fruits, pgs. 182–184
Wild Berry or Fruit Leather, pg. 184
As a substitute in Blackberry-Apple Crisp, pg. 21
As a variation in Mulberry Ripple Cheesecake, pg. 100
As a variation in Persimmon Smoothie, pg. 131

Quick ideas for using raspberries:
Scatter a handful on top of a mixed salad, especially one made with tender young greens. Serve with a blue cheese dressing or a mild vinaigrette.

ROSE HIPS *(Rosa* spp.*)*

Roses are found just about everywhere in the wild, and rose hips are easy to gather. Harvest hips when they are deeply colored and slightly soft; some foragers wait until after the first frost. Rose hips, especially the larger varieties, can be nibbled raw, but are more commonly dried to make tea, or stewed to make jam, jelly and other dishes. The fruits are loaded with vitamin C and other nutrients. The tiny seeds inside are rich in vitamin E (Steve Brill, *Identifying and Harvesting Edible and Medicinal Plants*), but they are also very bitter and may irritate the throat and stomach. If you're sampling a fresh hip, avoid eating the seeds or the dried blossom remnants.

Rose hips are so rich in vitamin C that they are used in the manufacture of some vitamin C capsules.

Most people remove the bitter seeds and surrounding hairs from rose hips before drying. To start, cut one hip in half from top to bottom; if you can easily scrape out the seeds, go ahead and process all remaining hips in this fashion, also removing the blossom remnants at the bottom. If the pulp is too sticky to remove the seeds easily, let the whole hips dry at room temperature for a few days, then try again. Don't let them get too dry, or the seeds will be even more difficult to remove. Dry split or whole hips (with the blossom remnants removed) at room temperature on a screen laid over a baking sheet, turning daily; or, dry in food dehydrator or 150°F oven (see pgs. 182– 184 for more information on dehydrating). Drying time depends on the size of the hips; split hips dry more quickly than whole hips. Store dried hips in tightly sealed glass jars in a dark location.

To make rose hip purée or juice, remove the stems and blossom ends, then measure the hips and place in a non-aluminum pot. For purée, add 1 cup water per quart of hips; for juice, add 3 cups water per quart of hips. (For a nice variation, use apple juice instead of water.) Heat to boiling, then reduce the heat; cover and simmer until soft, about 15 minutes, gently crushing the hips with a potato masher near the end of cooking.

For purée, process the cooked hips through a cone-shaped colander, or rub through a fine wire-mesh strainer; discard the seeds and skin. (I don't use a food mill with rose hips, because too many of the bitter seeds get into the purée.) **For juice,** transfer the mixture to a strainer lined with doubled, dampened cheesecloth and let it drip for 30 minutes; don't squeeze the fruit because some bitter seeds may get through the cheesecloth. Processed this way, a quart of rose hips will yield about 2 cups of lovely, pinkish-red purée, or about 2½ cups pinkish-red juice.

Rose Hip Tea
Per serving

Combine 1 tablespoon dried rose hips, or 2 tablespoons fresh rose hips, in a saucepan with 1 cup of cold water. Heat to boiling, then remove from heat, cover and let steep for 10 to 15 minutes. Strain and sweeten to taste with sugar, honey or maple syrup; serve with a lemon wedge if you like.

Rose Hip-Apple Jelly (no added pectin)

Tart apples add both flavor and pectin to this jelly.

½ pound fresh rose hips, blossom ends removed before weighing

½ pound Granny Smith apples, cored and chopped

1 lemon

2 cups sugar, approximate

Please read "Jelly Instructions for Fruits with Natural Pectin" on pg. 180 to learn about testing for doneness. In non-aluminum saucepan, combine rose hips and chopped apples. Add water to cover completely. Cut the lemon into quarters, and remove the rind (including the white pith) and seeds. Add lemon flesh to pan with rose hips. Heat to boiling over high heat. Reduce heat so mixture is simmering, then cover and simmer until all fruit is very soft, about 30 minutes. Mash with a potato masher.

Line a wire-mesh strainer with two thicknesses of damp cheesecloth; place over a non-aluminum pot. Spoon fruit mixture into cheesecloth; let drip for 2 hours without squeezing or stirring. At the end of the 2 hours, prepare 3 half-pint canning jars, bands and new lids as directed on pg. 185.

Discard pulp in cheesecloth. Measure the juice; you should have about 2½ cups. Place measured juice in a non-aluminum pot that holds 3 or 4 quarts. For each cup of juice, measure ⅞ cup of sugar. Heat juice to boiling over medium-high heat. Add sugar and cook, stirring constantly, until sugar dissolves. Increase heat to high and cook, skimming off any foam and stirring frequently, until jelly passes one or more of the doneness tests on pg. 166; this typically takes 10 to 15 minutes.

Once the jelly is done, skim any foam off the surface and pour it, while still hot, into the prepared canning jars; seal with prepared lids and bands. Process in a water-bath canner (pg. 185) for 10 minutes, or store in the refrigerator.

 One-half pound of slightly underripe crabapples can be substituted for the Granny Smith apples; remove the stems and blossom ends but don't bother removing the seeds. You could also substitute 2 cups of chopped wild apples.

Marlin with Rose Hip Glaze

4 servings

This sweet-tangy glaze would also be good with pork loin chops or tenderloin.

½ cup rose hip purée

3 tablespoons (packed) brown sugar

2 tablespoons Asian fish sauce

1 teaspoon butter

½ teaspoon finely minced fresh gingerroot

1 tablespoon freshly squeezed lime juice

4 pieces marlin, ¾ inch thick (6 to 8 ounces each)

1 tablespoon olive oil

In small non-aluminum saucepan, stir together purée, brown sugar, fish sauce, butter and gingerroot. Cook over medium heat, stirring frequently, until thickened, about 10 minutes. Transfer half of the sauce to a small bowl; stir in lime juice and set aside.

Heat oven to 400°F. Rinse fish; pat dry with paper towels. In heavy, oven-safe skillet, heat olive oil over medium-high heat until shimmering. Add fish in a single layer; cook for 2 minutes, then turn with spatula. Spread the mixture remaining in the saucepan evenly over each fish piece. Transfer skillet to oven; cook until the center is just opaque, 6 to 8 minutes. Transfer to serving plate. Serve with remaining sauce mixture.

Fish sauce is found in the Asian section of large supermarkets, or at specialty markets. I prefer Three Crabs brand from Vietnam; some excellent sauces also come from Thailand. The fish sauce adds a lot of flavor depth, but if you don't have any, substitute Japanese soy sauce such as Kikkoman.

Rose Hip Jelly (pectin added)

4 half-pints

2½ cups rose hip juice

¼ cup lemon juice

Half of a 1.75-ounce box powdered pectin

½ teaspoon butter, optional (helps reduce foaming)

2½ cups sugar

Prepare and process as directed in Jelly Instructions (using pectin), pg. 178.

Rose Hip Soup

This dish is common in the Scandinavian countries, where it is often served to soothe sore throats and colds. It can be served hot or cold; when served cold, it is sometimes diluted with water or apple juice and served as a beverage.

3 cups rose hip juice

2 tablespoons honey, or to taste

2 tablespoons freshly squeezed lemon juice, or to taste

¼ cup ground almonds

1 tablespoon potato starch, or 2 teaspoons cornstarch

1 tablespoon cold water

¼ cup sour cream

Fresh mint sprigs as a garnish

In a non-aluminum saucepan, combine rose hip juice, honey and lemon juice. Heat to boiling, then reduce heat and add ground almonds; simmer for about 5 minutes. In small bowl, blend potato starch and water, then whisk into simmering soup. Cook, whisking constantly, until mixture bubbles and thickens. Taste for seasoning, and adjust with more honey or lemon juice if you like. Divide mixture into 4 bowls. Add a tablespoon of sour cream to each serving; garnish with mint sprig.

Other recipes in this book featuring rose hips:
Six Recipes Using Wild Fruit Juice or Syrup, pgs. 172–176
Wild Berry or Fruit Syrup, pg. 177

Quick ideas for using rose hips:
Stir a few tablespoons of the purée into applesauce.
Mix 1 part rose hip juice with 2 parts apple juice; sweeten to taste, and serve as a breakfast drink.
Add a few tablespoons purée to the mixture when making a smoothie.
Use a mix of one part rose hip juice to three parts water when brewing black or green tea.

SERVICEBERRIES *(Amelanchier* spp.*)*

Found in one form or another throughout our area, serviceberries are surprisingly unfamiliar to many people. But the fruits are not showy, so they're easy to miss unless you're looking for them.

Technically a pome, serviceberries have a small crown on the bottom (like an apple), and several small, soft seeds. The seeds can be eaten with no trouble, and I never bother taking them out, but some cooks prefer to strain cooked serviceberries to remove the seeds. I typically use the fruits whole, in much the same way that I use blueberries or huckleberries. They're also a fantastic trail nibble; the sight of a laden serviceberry tree brings a smile to me when I'm hiking in the summer. They're sweet, with a subtle almond-like flavor, and they provide much-needed refreshment and energy on a hot July day.

Serviceberries were a staple in the diets of American Indians in our area, and were mentioned by explorers Meriwether Lewis and William Clark in the diaries of their western travels.

Even though many of the fruits are up out of reach, it's pretty easy to collect a good quantity of serviceberries if you find an area with several trees. Birds and other wildlife depend on serviceberries for food, so don't try too hard to get at the fruits you can't reach; leave them for the waxwings, robins and grosbeaks. (I have fond memories of picking serviceberries from a small tree that was heavy with them, and dodging the cedar waxwings that were gorging themselves on fruit just a few feet from me.)

Serviceberries can be used whole for baking, or turned into jam; they can also be dehydrated, for use in baked goods or trail mix. They are easy to freeze; wash the fruits and pat them dry, then spread on a baking sheet in a single layer. Freeze overnight, then transfer to plastic containers and seal tightly.

Serviceberry Pudding Cake

This is equally appropriate for breakfast or dessert. It's fabulous when still warm from the oven, but it's also good served at room temperature.

½ cup white sugar

3 tablespoons cold water

2 tablespoons lemon juice

1½ teaspoons cornstarch

2 cups fresh or frozen serviceberries (about 8 ounces)

1 cup all-purpose flour

½ cup (packed) golden brown sugar

2 teaspoons baking powder

1 teaspoon salt

1 egg

½ cup whole milk or buttermilk

6 tablespoons unsalted butter, melted and cooled slightly

1 teaspoon vanilla extract

Heat oven to 375°F. Spray an 8-inch-square baking dish with nonstick spray; set aside. In medium non-aluminum saucepan, stir together white sugar, water, lemon juice and cornstarch. Heat over medium heat, stirring constantly, until sugar dissolves, about 3 minutes. Add serviceberries; simmer for about a minute, stirring occasionally. Remove from heat.

In medium bowl, stir together flour, brown sugar, baking powder and salt. In large mixing bowl, combine egg, milk, butter and vanilla; beat with whisk until smooth. Add flour mixture; whisk until smooth. Scrape mixture into prepared baking dish, spreading evenly. Pour serviceberry mixture evenly over the top. Bake until a table knife inserted into the center comes out clean, about 30 minutes. Set pan on rack to cool for 5 or 10 minutes before serving. Cake can be cooled, then covered tightly with foil and kept at room temperature for up to 2 days.

Substitutions: Blueberries or huckleberries can be substituted for the serviceberries.

If using frozen serviceberries, measure them while still frozen, then rinse briefly under running water and spread out on a baking sheet lined with paper towels.

Serviceberry or Blueberry Freezer Jam   4 half-pints

This jam is easy to make because the fruit is not cooked; commercial pectin is cooked separately, then stirred into the fruit mixture.

1 quart serviceberries or blueberries

2 ¾ cups sugar

Two-thirds of a 1.75-ounce box powdered pectin (see pg. 178 for information on dividing pectin)

½ cup water

2 tablespoons lemon juice

Prepare 4 half-pint canning jars, bands and lids as described on pg. 185, or have clean plastic freezer containers ready (see tip below). Chop fruit to medium consistency in food processor (don't overprocess; jam should have small fruit chunks in it). Measure 1 ¾ cups chopped fruit; use any leftover fruit to top ice cream or cook in other recipes. Place measured fruit and the sugar in a large ceramic or Pyrex® mixing bowl. Stir well; set aside for 10 minutes, stirring several times with a wooden spoon.

After fruit has rested for 10 minutes, prepare pectin. In small non-aluminum saucepan, combine pectin, water and lemon juice; stir well (mixture may be lumpy). Heat to a full, rolling boil over high heat, stirring constantly. Cook at a rolling boil for 1 minute, stirring constantly. Pour pectin mixture into fruit in bowl. Stir constantly with a wooden spoon until sugar is completely dissolved and no longer grainy, about 3 minutes; a few grains may remain, but the mixture should no longer look cloudy (or the jam will be cloudy).

Pour into prepared jars or containers, leaving ½ inch headspace; cover with clean lids. Let stand at room temperature for 24 hours; the jam should set (it may be softer than regular jam, especially at first; that's okay). If jam is not set, refrigerate for several days until set before using or freezing. Use within 3 weeks, or freeze until needed; thaw frozen jam in refrigerator.

 Special plastic containers, designed especially for freezing jelly and jam, are available with the canning supplies at the supermarket.

Serviceberry and Ricotta Brunch Ring 12 to 16 servings

This delicious cake gets extra moistness from ricotta cheese. The almonds add a nice texture, and point up the subtly nutty taste of the serviceberries.

½ cup (1 stick) unsalted butter, softened

1 cup sugar

1 container (15 ounces) ricotta cheese (reduced-fat works fine)

½ cup whole or 2% milk

2 eggs

1 teaspoon vanilla extract

2½ cups flour

1 tablespoon baking powder

½ teaspoon salt

1½ cups fresh serviceberries (about 6½ ounces)

1 cup finely chopped slivered almonds (about 4½ ounces)

Powdered sugar for dusting, optional

Heat oven to 350°F. Grease and flour a 12-cup bundt pan or an angel-food cake pan; set aside.

In large mixing bowl, cream butter with electric mixer for about 1 minute. Add sugar; beat for another minute. Add ricotta cheese, milk, eggs and vanilla; beat on medium speed for 2 minutes, scraping bowl several times. Combine flour, baking powder and salt in sifter or wire-mesh strainer; sift or shake mixture into mixing bowl. Add serviceberries and almonds, and stir together with wooden spoon until well mixed.

Spoon mixture into prepared pan, evening out and smoothing the top. Bake in center of oven until a toothpick inserted into the center comes out clean, about an hour. Cool on a wire rack for 20 minutes, then remove from pan; put the prettiest side up. Dust top with powdered sugar, if you like. Cool until just warm before slicing, or cool completely and serve at room temperature.

 If you have leftovers, wrap tightly in plastic wrap, then wrap again in foil, smoothing tightly. Seal the seams with freezer tape, and freeze up to 3 months.

Serviceberry and Wild Rice Muffins

6 muffins

Wild rice is a natural with serviceberries in these hearty muffins.

3/4 **cup all-purpose flour**

1/4 **cup sugar**

1 teaspoon baking powder

1/4 **teaspoon salt**

1/2 **cup fresh or previously frozen serviceberries (about 2 ounces)**

1/4 **cup whole or 2% milk**

2 tablespoons butter, melted and cooled slightly

1 egg

1/3 **cup cooked wild rice**

Heat oven to 350°F. Line 6-cup muffin pan with paper liners, or spray with nonstick spray; set aside. Place wire-mesh strainer over large mixing bowl. Add flour, sugar, baking powder and salt; shake into bowl to sift together. Place serviceberries in small bowl; spoon about 2 teaspoons of the flour mixture over them, stirring to coat.

In measuring cup, beat together milk, butter and egg. Pour milk mixture into flour mixture and fold together with rubber spatula. Add floured serviceberries and wild rice; fold together. Spoon into prepared muffin cups. Bake until lightly browned and a toothpick inserted into the center of a muffin comes out clean, 25 to 30 minutes.

Serviceberry Filling

About 1/2 cup; easily increased

1 teaspoon water

1/2 **teaspoon cornstarch**

5 1/2 **ounces fresh or previously serviceberries (about 1 1/4 cups)**

1/4 **cup sugar**

1 tablespoon grated apple

In small bowl, blend together water and cornstarch; set aside. In small, heavy-bottomed saucepan, combine serviceberries, sugar and apple. Crush fruit gently with a potato masher to start juices flowing. Heat to boiling over medium-high heat, then cook, stirring frequently and mashing once more, until mixture is no longer runny; this will take 7 to 9 minutes. Add cornstarch mixture, stirring constantly; cook for about 1½ minutes longer, or until thick. Cool before using.

Use this to prepare Easy Bear Claws (pg. 30), Fruit-Striped Cookie Fingers (pg. 145), or Fruit-Filled Muffins (pg. 163). Refrigerate extra filling, and use to top oatmeal or toast.

Serviceberry Pie
1 pie (6 to 8 servings)

Chopped almonds add a wonderful texture to this luscious pie.

3 cups fresh or previously frozen serviceberries, divided (12 to 13 ounces)

⅔ cup sugar

3 tablespoons cornstarch

1 tablespoon lemon juice

1 tablespoon butter, cut into several pieces

½ teaspoon cinnamon

A pinch of salt

A few drops almond extract, optional

Ready-to-use pastry for double-crust pie

⅓ cup finely chopped almonds

1 egg yolk, beaten with 1 tablespoon cold water

In medium non-aluminum saucepan, combine 1 cup of serviceberries with the sugar, cornstarch and lemon juice; stir to mix. Heat to boiling over medium heat, stirring constantly; cook, stirring constantly, until liquid clears and thickens. Remove from heat; stir in butter, cinnamon, salt and extract. Let cool for about 5 minutes, then add remaining 2 cups serviceberries and set aside until completely cool, about 1 hour.

When the serviceberry mixture has cooled, heat oven to 400°F. Fit one pastry into ungreased pie plate. Scatter almonds evenly in crust. Scrape cooled serviceberry mixture into pie plate. Moisten edges of pastry in pie plate with a little cold water, then top with second pastry. Seal, trim and flute edges. Cut 6 to 8 inch-long slits in the crust. Place pie on baking sheet (to catch drips). Brush top with beaten egg. Bake until crust is golden and filling bubbles through slits, about 30 minutes. Transfer to rack to cool; best served warm.

Microwave Oatmeal with Serviceberries and Nuts

Easy, quick and filling, this is the perfect breakfast.

²/₃ cup water

⅓ cup old-fashioned rolled oats

2 to 3 tablespoons fresh serviceberries

2 drops of vanilla extract

1 tablespoon chopped pecans

Honey, maple syrup or brown sugar to taste

Cream or whole milk to taste, optional

In microwave-safe bowl that holds 2 to 3 cups, combine water, oats, serviceberries and vanilla. Microwave on high, uncovered, until oatmeal is thick and most of the water has been absorbed, 1½ to 2½ minutes. Remove bowl from microwave; stir well and let stand until all water is absorbed, 30 seconds to 1 minute. Sprinkle with pecans; top with honey and cream to taste.

Prepare this one bowl at a time; cooking times will change if you put two or more in the microwave at the same time. Use old-fashioned rolled oatmeal, rather than quick-cooking oatmeal, for the best texture.

Other recipes in this book featuring serviceberries:
Refrigerator Cookies with Dried Berries, pg. 15
Fruits of the Forest Pie, pg. 170
Dehydrating Wild Berries and Fruits, pgs. 182–184
Wild Berry or Fruit Leather, pg. 184
As a substitute in Blackberry-Apple Crisp, pg. 21
As a substitute in Blueberry Streusel Muffins, pg. 31
As a substitute in Individual Currant Cheesecakes, pg. 55
As a variation in Persimmon Smoothie, pg. 131

Quick ideas for using serviceberries:
Substitute serviceberries for fresh blueberries in recipes. Serviceberries are not quite as juicy as blueberries, so you may need to increase the liquid slightly. Use 1¼ cups of serviceberries in place of one of the sliced apples when making apple pie.

SPICEBUSH, NORTHERN *(Lindera benzoin)*

If you encounter a spicebush shrub in the woods, you'll know it; the entire plant has a pleasantly spicy smell that is similar to allspice. The berries—technically drupes—can be used as a substitute for allspice, either whole or ground. They work well in chutney, marinades, jam and sauces. Even the leaves can be dried, then used to flavor stews and marinades; they have a more subtle flavor than the fruits.

The fruits tend to develop a musty flavor if stored at room temperature for more than a few weeks; for best results, keep them in the refrigerator or freezer until needed. For ground spicebush, use a coffee grinder or mortar and pestle to grind them just before use; the ground spice loses its flavor quickly.

Jerk Marinade
Enough marinade for 2 to 3 pounds meat

"Jerk" cooking is a Caribbean specialty that uses a spicy, highly seasoned marinade to flavor cuts like flank steak. Here's a jerk-style marinade that uses spicebush berries; the heat has been toned down a bit, so if you like really spicy jerk, substitute habañero peppers for the jalapeño peppers.

¼ cup freshly squeezed lime juice

¼ cup vegetable oil

2 tablespoons soy sauce

2 tablespoons molasses

2 teaspoons fresh thyme leaves, or 1 teaspoon dried

1 teaspoon coarse black pepper

12 whole spicebush berries

3 cloves garlic

2 green onions, cut into 1-inch pieces (discard roots)

1 or 2 jalapeño peppers, stems and seeds removed

1-inch cube of peeled fresh gingerroot

Combine all ingredients in blender; process until smooth.

To use, combine marinade and meat in heavy zipper-style plastic bag; seal and turn to coat meat with marinade. Marinate in refrigerator, turning occasionally. Flank steak or pork roast should be marinated at least 4 hours, and as long as overnight; pork chops or chicken pieces should be marinated 2 to 4 hours. After marinating, remove meat from marinade and broil or grill over direct, high heat. Discard marinade.

Spicy Plum Chutney

About 1½ cups

This is delicious alongside grilled or broiled meats and fish, and with curry dishes.

4 whole cardamom pods

6 whole spicebush berries

3 cups cut-up plum pieces (½-inch pieces), wild or domestic

¾ cup diced onion (¼-inch dice)

1 cup diced red bell pepper (¼-inch dice)

¼ cup golden raisins or purchased dried currants

¼ cup (packed) brown sugar

¼ cup balsamic vinegar or red-wine vinegar

1 tablespoon minced crystallized ginger (found in the spice aisle)

½ teaspoon yellow mustard seeds

½ teaspoon salt

¼ teaspoon hot red pepper flakes

Split cardamom pods and transfer seeds to mortar; add spicebush and crush until mixture is coarse. Combine spice mixture with remaining ingredients in heavy-bottomed non-aluminum saucepan. Heat to boiling over high heat. Reduce heat so mixture simmers steadily and cook until thickened and syrupy, about 45 minutes. Stir frequently, especially near the end of the cooking time, to prevent sticking. Cool and transfer to a clean pint jar; store in refrigerator for up to 3 weeks.

Substitutions: If you have wild plums but no spicebush berries, substitute 2 whole allspice berries, or ¼ teaspoon ground allspice, for the spicebush berries. You could also substitute wild cherries for the plums (if you have the patience to pit 3 cups!).

Quick ideas for using spicebush:

Substitute whole spicebush berries for whole allspice in recipes; use twice as many spicebush berries as the quantity listed for allspice.

Add a few whole spicebush berries to marinades for beef, pork or venison.

When making applesauce, add 3 or 4 whole spicebush berries to the apples during cooking. If you're straining or puréeing the applesauce after cooking, leave the berries in the mixture; otherwise, fish them out with a spoon afterwards.

STRAWBERRIES *(Fragaria virginiana, F. vesca)*

It's fun to watch the reaction of someone who's tasting a wild strawberry for the first time. Wonderment over the tiny size of the fruit changes to awed delight when they taste it. "I never knew strawberries could taste like this!" is a common response— quickly followed by a dive to the ground in search of more strawberries.

Wild strawberries are so tiny that it is hard to gather enough to make, say, a batch of jam—and they're so good that it's tough to stop eating them rather than putting them in the berry pail. I've never made wild strawberry jelly, because I've never wanted to sacrifice enough berries to make juice. However, if you've hit the strawberry jackpot and want to make jelly (or other recipes prepared with juice), follow the instructions for making mulberry juice on pg. 98.

The hardest part about picking enough wild strawberries to make jam is refraining from devouring them on the spot.

When you're using wild strawberries in recipes that were written for domestic berries, don't rely on per-cup measurements. Wild strawberries are so much smaller than their domesticated cousins that they pack more tightly into the cup, so you'd be using more strawberries (by weight) than the recipe intended. Domestic strawberries are also less juicy, so liquid may need to be reduced when substituting wild strawberries.

Wild strawberries can be frozen, but they will be soft when thawed. Spread them in a single layer on a baking sheet lined with waxed paper. Freeze overnight, then pack into tightly sealed plastic containers and store in the coldest part of the freezer.

Strawberry Filling
About ½ cup; easily increased

½ teaspoon water

½ teaspoon cornstarch

6 ounces fresh or previously frozen wild strawberries (about 1 cup)

2 teaspoons sugar

1 teaspoon lemon juice

In small bowl, blend together water and cornstarch; set aside. In small, heavy-bottomed non-aluminum saucepan, combine strawberries, sugar and lemon juice. Crush fruit gently with a potato masher to start juices flowing. Heat to boiling over medium-high heat, then cook, stirring frequently, until mixture is no longer runny; this will take 8 to 10 minutes. Add cornstarch mixture, stirring constantly; cook for about 1 minute longer, or until thick. Cool before using.

Use this to prepare Easy Bear Claws (pg. 30), Fruit-Striped Cookie Fingers (pg. 145), or Fruit-Filled Muffins (pg. 163). Refrigerate extra filling, and use to top oatmeal or toast.

Strawberry Freezer Jam

4 half-pints

Freezer jam is not cooked, so it has a fresher taste and a vibrant color. It is a little softer than cooked jam. Wild strawberries make the best freezer jam in the world, but if you can't bear to part with enough to make a full batch of this, see below for small-batch instructions.

1¼ pounds fresh wild strawberries (about 3½ cups)

4 cups sugar

1 pouch Certo® liquid pectin

2 tablespoons freshly squeezed lemon juice

Wash and hull strawberries. Pulse on-and-off in a food processor until fruit is finely chopped (not puréed); if you prefer, mash with a potato masher. Measure finely chopped strawberries; transfer exactly 2 cups to a large ceramic or Pyrex® mixing bowl. If you have any leftover chopped strawberries, enjoy them over ice cream; don't use more than 2 cups for this recipe.

Add sugar and stir well; set aside for 10 minutes, stirring several times with a wooden spoon. Meanwhile, stir pectin and lemon juice together in a small bowl. After strawberries and sugar have stood for 10 minutes, add pectin mixture to strawberries, scraping to get all the pectin into the berries. Stir continuously for 3 minutes; sugar should be completely dissolved. Cover bowl tightly with plastic wrap. Let stand at room temperature for 24 hours; jam should be softly set.

When jam has set for 24 hours, prepare 4 half-pint canning jars, bands and lids as described on pg. 185, or have clean plastic freezer containers ready (see tip below). Divide fruit between prepared containers, leaving ½ inch headspace. Cover and refrigerate. Use within 3 weeks, or freeze until needed; thaw frozen jam in refrigerator.

Special plastic containers, designed especially for freezing, are available with the canning supplies at the supermarket.

Small-Batch Strawberry Freezer Jam

If you don't have enough berries to make a full batch, you can make a half-batch. The only tricky part is measuring half of the pectin. It is extremely thick and clings to the measuring spoon or cup, making accurate measuring difficult. To make it easier, mix up the full batch of pectin and lemon juice in a measuring cup, then use exactly half of that in the strawberry mixture. The lemon juice makes it easier to measure.

Place 1 cup of finely chopped strawberries into a large mixing bowl. Add 2 cups sugar; stir and let stand as directed above. Mix the full pouch of pectin with 2 tablespoons lemon juice in a glass measuring cup (when I tested it, it came out to ½ cup, but the pectin formula may change in the future so you need to check this each time). After strawberries and sugar have stood for 10 minutes, pour *exactly half* of the pectin mixture into the strawberry mixture (I poured pectin into the strawberry mixture until there was ¼ cup left in the measuring cup). Proceed as directed. Discard remaining pectin if you don't have another use for it.

Fruit-Filled Muffins
12 muffins

These make a nice, quick breakfast. Freeze any muffins you won't be eating within a few days, wrapping them tightly in plastic wrap and then in foil.

1³/₄ cups all-purpose flour

½ to ²/₃ cup sugar, depending on how sweet you want the muffins

2 teaspoons baking powder

¼ teaspoon salt

²/₃ cup whole or 2% milk

¹/₃ cup vegetable oil

1 egg

1 teaspoon vanilla extract

½ cup Strawberry Filling (pg. 161), or other wild fruit filling (see "Filling options" below)

Heat oven to 375°F. Line a 12-cup muffin tin with paper liners, or spray with nonstick spray; set aside. Place wire-mesh strainer over large mixing bowl. Add flour, sugar, baking powder and salt; shake strainer to sift mixture into bowl. In measuring cup or small bowl, beat together milk, oil, egg and vanilla. Add milk mixture to flour mixture; stir with a wooden spoon until just moistened. Spoon half of the batter evenly into prepared muffin cups. Drop about 1 teaspoon of the filling onto the center of the muffin batter, keeping away from the edges; spoon remaining batter over filling. Bake until golden brown and springy to the touch, 20 to 25 minutes.

Filling options: This recipe works with any of the following fillings: Apple or Crabapple (pg. 9), Blackberry (pg. 20), Blackhaw (pg. 27), Blueberry (pg. 33), Green Gooseberry (pg. 67), Ground Cherry (pg. 76), Mulberry (pg. 101), Muscadine (pg. 107), Peach (pg. 119), Pear (pg. 123), Persimmon (pg. 129), Plum (pg. 137), Raspberry (pg. 143), Serviceberry (pg. 156), or Strawberry (pg. 161). You may also use plain, unsweetened mashed pawpaws as a filling.

Mixed Greens with Strawberries, Honey Pecans and Blue Cheese

4 first-course servings; easily increased

Here's a salad with a fabulous combination of flavors and textures. It serves four as a first course for a special dinner, or two if presented as the center item for a luncheon. If you like, you can prepare the nuts a day or two in advance.

Honey pecans:

¾ cup pecan halves

1 tablespoon honey

2 teaspoons butter, melted

A pinch of curry powder

Salad:

3 slices thick-cut bacon

6 cups tender mixed salad greens

3 thin slices red onion, quartered after slicing

½ cup blue cheese crumbles

⅔ to ¾ cup fresh wild strawberries (4 to 5 ounces)

½ cup prepared balsamic vinegar dressing, or to taste

Prepare the nuts: Heat oven to 425°F. Line a small baking sheet with foil; spray with nonstick spray. In a small bowl, stir together the pecans, honey, butter and curry powder. Spread out on foil-lined baking sheet. Bake until nuts are lightly browned, 5 to 7 minutes, stirring twice. Remove from oven before they are as brown as you would like because they will continue to cook for a few minutes after you remove them from the oven. Let nuts cool completely; can be prepared a day or two in advance (store cooled nuts in air-tight container at room temperature).

To assemble the salad, shortly before serving, cut the bacon crosswise (across the width) into ⅜-inch pieces. In medium skillet, fry over medium heat until crisp, stirring frequently. Transfer with slotted spoon to a plate lined with paper towels; blot surface with another paper towel.

Divide greens evenly between 4 salad-sized serving plates, or 2 dinner-sized plates. Sprinkle evenly with onions, breaking up the rings a bit. Top with bacon; sprinkle cheese over the bacon. Carefully place the strawberries on top, arranging attractively. Scatter honey pecans over all. Drizzle dressing over salads. Serve immediately.

Strawberries and Shortbread   4 servings

This simple, but interesting, dessert was inspired by a recipe from the well-known French chef, Jacques Pépin.

2 cups fresh wild strawberries (about 12 ounces), divided

2 teaspoons sugar, or to taste

¼ teaspoon vanilla extract

4 ounces shortbread cookies

⅓ cup crème fraîche or sour cream

2 tablespoons (packed) brown sugar

4 sprigs fresh mint for garnish, optional

In mini food processor, process half of the strawberries with the sugar and vanilla; transfer to small bowl. Slice remaining strawberries, then gently stir into the strawberry purée. Place shortbread cookies in plastic bag, and crush coarsely with rolling pin. (If preparing in advance, cover and refrigerate strawberries until serving time; set crushed cookies aside.)

To serve, spoon about 2 tablespoons of the strawberry mixture into each of 4 wine glasses or parfait dishes. Divide shortbread crumbs evenly among glasses. Top evenly with remaining strawberry mixture. Spoon crème fraîche evenly on top; sprinkle with brown sugar and garnish with mint sprig. Let stand 5 to 10 minutes before serving.

Other recipes in this book featuring wild strawberries:
    Refrigerator Cookies with Dried Berries, pg. 15
    Wild Berry Vinegar, pg. 19
    Strawberry-Gooseberry Dessert Sauce, pg. 69
    Dehydrating Wild Berries and Fruits, pgs. 182–184
    Wild Berry or Fruit Leather, pg. 184
    As a substitute in Wild Blueberry Pancakes, pg. 34
    As a variation in Persimmon Smoothie, pg. 131
    As a substitute in Raspberry Dip, pg. 143

Quick ideas for using wild strawberries:
    Sprinkle over cold cereal before adding milk and sugar; way better
        than sliced bananas!
    Add to mixed fruit salads.
    Add a few to an apple pie, for a delightful difference.
    Enjoy them over ice cream, or in a bowl with a little cream or yogurt.

SUMAC: SMOOTH, STAGHORN, FRAGRANT and WINGED (Rhus glabra, R. typhina, R. aromatica and R. copallinum)

Smooth and staghorn trees are the most familiar members of the sumac family, but fragrant sumac, which grows as a shrub rather than a tree, is also found in our area; it has fuzzy, reddish-orange fruits that can be used in the same way as the larger, pyramid-shaped clusters found on smooth and staghorn sumac. Winged sumac is a small tree or large shrub; its fruit clusters are similar to those of smooth or staghorn sumac, but the fruits are purplish or maroon.

Sumac is probably the first unfamiliar wild edible that kids learn about. "Sumac-ade" is a staple at summer camps across our area; it's easy for kids to identify and pick the bright reddish-orange clusters, and fun to make a tasty beverage out of them.

Fragrant and winged sumac fruits are ripe in midsummer, usually before smooth and staghorn sumac. All should be harvested when they're fully ripe and a bit sticky; if you wait too long, rain will wash away the flavor. Use a pruning snips to cut off entire clusters; it doesn't hurt the plant, because they reproduce by underground runners.

When working with staghorn, smooth and winged sumac, you can use the whole cluster, or pick the berries off the stems; picking is more work, but it eliminates any dirt, spiders or other undesirables that may be hiding inside the cluster. For storage, freeze picked berries in heavy plastic bags; the frozen berries retain all their flavor and can be used later to make sumac juice, tea or whatever you like. Clusters can be frozen as well, but they take up more room; as an option, place them in a loosely sealed paper bag and let them dry, then use them to make tea (they won't make very good juice after they've been dried). Sumac berries have tiny hairs that are somewhat irritating to the throat; they can be removed by straining the liquid through a paper coffee filter.

To make sumac juice, use fresh berry clusters that are still sticky; frozen berries or clusters work as well, as long as they were sticky before freezing. Place clusters or picked berries in a soup pot or plastic bucket, then add cold water just to cover. Squeeze the berries with your hands, and rub them up and down along the sides of the pot as though scrubbing on a washboard. Do this for a few minutes, then let the mixture stand for a few minutes and repeat. I usually let them soak for 10 to 20 minutes after that; I want to extract as much flavor as possible. Strain the mixture through a wire-mesh strainer, then again through a paper coffee filter. Sweeten to taste, and serve cold as a lemonade-type beverage; or, use the unsweetened liquid in recipes.

For stronger sumac juice, you can reduce it to approximately half-volume by cooking (however, you are eliminating much of the vitamin C by heating it). Or, add more sumac clusters to already prepared sumac juice and repeat the juice-making process to get a stronger liquid.

Caution: People who are highly allergic to poison ivy, mangoes or cashews should avoid all sumacs, which are in the same family and may cause a severe allergic reaction.

Cedar-Planked Salmon with Sumac-Maple Glaze

4 to 6 servings

Cooking salmon on cedar planks is traditional in the Pacific Northwest. In this version, the salmon is topped with a tangy-sweet glaze made from sumac juice and maple syrup.

Red cedar plank, about ½ inch thick and large enough to hold fish

1 cup strained sumac juice

1-inch chunk peeled fresh gingerroot

1 clove garlic

2 strips orange zest (colored rind only, with none of the white pith), each about 2 inches long by ½ inch wide

¾ cup pure maple syrup (don't use substitutes in this recipe)

1 tablespoon soy sauce

2 teaspoons butter

2-pound fillet of salmon, skin on

Salt and freshly ground pepper

In a clean bucket, soak plank in water to cover for 8 hours or overnight; weight with clean rocks to keep plank submerged. When you're ready to start cooking, prepare the glaze: In small, heavy-bottomed non-aluminum saucepan, boil sumac juice over high heat until reduced to about ⅓ cup (see "Reducing Liquid," pg. 45). While the sumac juice is cooking, chop the gingerroot, garlic and orange zest until fine in a food processor.

When the sumac juice is reduced, add the chopped gingerroot mixture, the maple syrup and soy sauce. Continue boiling until reduced slightly, about 5 minutes. Remove from heat and stir in butter; set aside until cooled to room temperature. While glaze is cooling, prepare grill for direct, high heat (see "Grilling: Direct vs. Indirect Heat," pg. 27). Drain plank and pat dry. Place salmon on plank, skin-side down; season to taste with salt and pepper. Reserve half of the glaze; brush fish with remaining glaze. Place plank on grill grate directly over heat. Cover grill and cook until fish is just opaque, 15 to 25 minutes depending on the thickness of the fish. (The plank may catch fire around the edges near the end of cooking time; don't worry about it unless it gets too strong. If necessary, douse the edges with a spray bottle of water.) When the salmon is almost done, warm reserved sauce over medium heat, then transfer to a small serving bowl. Serve salmon on plank, or transfer fish to a serving platter; pass warmed sauce with the fish. Discard the plank after use.

 Buy untreated cedar from the lumberyard, or look at a specialty shop or upscale grocer for planks that are marketed specifically for cooking.

Sumac Tea

Sumac makes a pleasant hot tea that is slightly tart, with floral overtones. It's similar to chamomile tea, or to a mild version of the commercial herbal-tea blend called Red Zinger.

4 good-sized sumac clusters, or about 1 cup of picked berries

4 cups water

Honey or sugar to taste, optional

Rinse the sumac clusters briefly, and set aside to drain. Heat water to boiling in saucepan; remove from heat and set aside to cool for about 5 minutes. While water is cooling, cut smaller clusters away from woody stems, discarding stems. Add clusters or picked berries to hot water and let stand for 5 minutes. Use potato masher or large wooden spoon to bruise the sumac; you don't want to crack the seeds doing this, so don't use too much force. Let stand for about 5 minutes longer, then strain through a damp tea towel or several layers of cheesecloth. Serve warm or cold, adding sweetening to taste if you like.

Variation: Sumac-Mint Tea
Add a few fresh mint leaves to the hot water with the sumac.

If you want iced tea, chill the brewed tea for an hour before serving. I like hot sumac tea unsweetened, but you can add sugar or honey to taste if you prefer; iced tea tastes better if sweetened lightly. Iced sumac tea is best the day it is made; it begins to turn an unappetizing brown after a day in the refrigerator.

Other recipes in this book featuring sumac:
Elderberry-Sumac Jelly, pg. 63

WINTERGREEN *(Gaultheria procumbens)*

This cheerful-looking plant is a welcome sight in the woods from fall through winter. All parts have a spicy, minty smell and taste; ripe red berries make a wonderfully refreshing trail nibble. It's hard to gather them in large quantities, but I've read that some foragers gather enough to make preserves from them.

Leaves may be used to make tea, which is used to relieve upset stomach; in fact, wintergreen is sometimes referred to as "teaberry" because it is so often used in this way. Pour boiling water over handful of leaves and let it steep for about 15 minutes.

Caution: Wintergreen fruits and leaves contain methyl salicylate, an aspirin-like compound. Persons who are sensitive to aspirin should not ingest any part of these plants.

Wintergreen Malt   2 servings

This is a delightful malt, with a clean, refreshing taste. It's a good use for a small harvest of these berries.

2 to 3 heaping scoops vanilla ice cream

1½ cups whole milk, very cold

3 tablespoons malted milk powder

2 to 3 tablespoons wintergreen berries

4 sugar wafers, optional

Combine all ingredients except wafers in blender. Cover tightly and pulse on-and-off several times, until ingredients are beginning to mix and have filled the bottom of the blender. Blend on regular setting until desired consistency, 30 to 45 seconds. Divide between 2 chilled malt glasses; tuck 2 wafers into each malt and serve immediately.

Quick ideas for using wintergreen berries:
Scatter a few on top of ice cream for a minty sundae.
Mash a handful of berries and add to applesauce.

MIXED BERRY DISHES

Following are two very special recipes that use a mixed bag of wild berries or fruits. Substitutions are given for some of the ingredients, in case you are missing one of the species listed.

Fruits of the Forest Pie

1 pie (6 to 8 servings)

This uses a mixture of brambles and berries—heaven in a pie crust. Use what you have on hand (or in the freezer) to fill the amounts noted. Use crabapples, hawthorns or domestic apples for the apple portion; be sure to remove all seeds and blossom remnants if using crabapples or haws.

Ready-to-use pastry for two-crust pie

1½ cups blueberries, serviceberries or huckleberries— all one type, or a mix

1½ cups brambles such as raspberries (red, black or purple-flowering), blackberries or good-quality dewberries—all one type, or a mix

½ cup grated apple, crabapple or hawthorn

¾ to 1 cup sugar, depending on the sweetness of the berries

1 tablespoon cornstarch

1 tablespoon butter, cut into small pieces

Optional wash: 1 egg lightly beaten with 1 tablespoon milk

Heat oven to 400°F. Line pie plate with one crust; set aside. In mixing bowl, combine berries, brambles, apple, sugar and cornstarch; stir gently to combine. Spoon into bottom crust. Scatter cut-up butter over the fruit. Brush crust edges lightly with water; top with second crust, crimping edges to seal (or, make a lattice crust; see "Making a Lattice-Top Pie," pg. 171). Brush crust with egg mixture; cut several slits in crust. Place pie on a baking sheet (to catch drips). Bake for 10 minutes, then reduce heat to 350°F and cook until crust is rich golden brown and filling bubbles through slits, 35 to 45 minutes longer. Cool on wire rack; best served slightly warm, the day it is made.

Brambleberry Cream Sauce
About 2 cups (enough for 6 to 8 servings)

Serve this sauce warm with crêpes, over angel food cake or biscuits, on cereal or pancakes, or however you like.

4 tablespoons (half of a stick) cold unsalted butter, divided

2 tablespoons all-purpose flour

1 cup heavy cream

$^2/_3$ cup sugar

$^1/_4$ teaspoon salt

$^3/_4$ cup red raspberries, purple-flowering raspberries or red dewberries—all one type, or a mix

$^3/_4$ cup black raspberries, blackberries or black dewberries— all one type, or a mix

In heavy-bottomed saucepan, melt 2 tablespoons of the butter over medium heat. Whisk in flour. Cook, whisking constantly, until mixture thickens and turns golden; don't let it burn. Whisk in cream, sugar and salt. Cook over medium heat, whisking frequently, until mixture bubbles and thickens to saucelike consistency; this will take 3 or 4 minutes. Stir in berries. Cook, stirring gently a few times, for about a minute. Remove from heat. Quickly cut remaining butter into 4 pieces. Add a piece to the warm sauce and stir until it melts. Repeat with remaining butter, adding just 1 piece at a time and stirring until it melts. Serve immediately, or keep warm until ready to serve.

Making a Lattice-Top Pie
When you're making a pie with a top crust, you can use a lattice top in place of the standard, full top crust; the lattice looks very pretty and homestyle. Here's how.

Fit the bottom crust as usual, and add the filling. Cut the second pastry into ½-inch-wide strips. Position a row of strips, running vertically across the top of the pie and separated by ½ inch. Now begin to weave a row of strips horizontally across the top of the pie, lifting the vertical strips over the horizontal strips in an alternating pattern. Trim all strips even with the edge of the overhanging crust, and pinch all edges very well to seal; flute edge decoratively. Brush with egg wash or any other finish as directed in the recipe; the pie is ready to be baked.

SIX RECIPES USING
WILD FRUIT JUICE or SYRUP

Here are a half-dozen recipes that work well with juice or syrup you've made from just about any type of wild fruit. One or two suggested juices are listed with most recipes, but feel free to experiment, substituting a different type of juice for the one listed. You may need to increase the amount of sweetening if your juice is particularly tart.

Wild Fruit Sorbet

About 3 cups

This basic recipe works with any wild fruit juice in this book, except mountain ash; you need an ice-cream maker to prepare this. Depending on the type of fruit juice you use, your sorbet may be pink, purple, rich purple, greenish or red. For an attractive presentation, place a small scoop of the sorbet in a dish with a small scoop of lemon sherbet and another of vanilla ice cream; garnish with a shortbread or ginger cookie.

1 cup sugar

⅝ cup water

1¾ cups blackberry juice or other wild fruit juice

A pinch of salt

1 egg white (from commercially pasteurized egg if concerned about salmonella)

If using ice-cream maker that requires pre-freezing, place it in freezer as directed by manufacturer, generally 12 to 24 hours. Combine sugar and water in small saucepan. Heat to boiling, stirring just until sugar dissolves. Remove from heat; cool to room temperature, then place in freezer for 30 minutes, or in refrigerator for at least 2 hours, until completely chilled. Combine sugar mixture, wild fruit juice and salt in a 1-quart jar; chill overnight.

Transfer mixture to prepared ice-cream maker and churn until slushy and beginning to hold a soft shape, 7 to 10 minutes. In small bowl, beat egg white with a fork for 45 seconds, then add to ice cream maker with slush. Continue to churn until mixture freezes to a soft ice-cream consistency, 12 to 15 minutes longer. The sorbet will be very soft at this point. Scoop sorbet into plastic container and freeze for at least 3 hours; mixture can be frozen for up to a week. It will remain scoopable for several days; if it becomes too hard to scoop, place container in the refrigerator for about 30 minutes to soften the sorbet slightly before serving.

Wild Fruit Gels (Gumdrops)

This works great with the juice from any wild fruit in this book, except mountain ash. Juice from dark fruits like chokecherries, raspberries or blackberries makes attractive, deeply colored gels; for example, juice from highbush cranberries makes stunning, bright-red gels. Note: This is based on a recipe that appeared in Family Circle *magazine in the early 1970s. I've cut the recipe in half; if you want to make a full batch, simply double the ingredients and use an 8-inch-square baking dish.*

Half of a 1.75-ounce box powdered pectin (see pg. 178 for information on dividing pectin)

⅜ cup wild fruit juice

¼ teaspoon baking soda

½ cup sugar, plus additional for rolling the gels

½ cup white corn syrup

You'll need two medium saucepans (large, if you're doubling the recipe), two long-handled spoons and a standard-sized loaf pan (glass or nonstick metal work best). Wet the inside of the loaf pan, then line it with plastic wrap, smoothing it out (the water helps hold the wrap in place).

Combine the pectin, fruit juice and baking soda in one pan; combine the ½ cup sugar and the corn syrup in the other. Place a spoon in each pan, and keep those spoons separate from one another throughout the procedure.

Stir both mixtures well, and place both pans over medium-high heat. The pectin mixture will foam up at the beginning; stirring will prevent it from boiling over. Cook both mixtures, stirring alternately, until the foam subsides from the pectin mixture and the sugar mixture is boiling vigorously, about 5 minutes. Pour the pectin mixture in a thin, steady stream into the sugar mixture, stirring constantly. Boil the mixture, stirring constantly, for 1 minute longer. Pour the mixture immediately into the loaf pan. Let stand at room temperature, covered very loosely with a piece of cheesecloth to discourage flies, until completely cool; this will take about 2 hours. (Alternately, you can pour the mixture into tiny molds, if you have them.) Place another piece of plastic wrap on top, pressing it against the surface of the mixture; refrigerate for at least 3 hours and as long as overnight.

Unmold gelled mixture onto a cutting board; remove plastic wrap. Cut into 1-inch squares with a sharp knife (dip it in very hot water, then dry off, to make cutting easier). Roll gels in sugar, and arrange in a single layer on a serving plate. Refrigerate or freeze for longer storage, keeping a little space between gels and using waxed paper between layers.

Panna Cotta with Fruit Gel Topping

6 servings

Panna cotta means "cooked cream"; it's an elegant but simple Italian dessert. You'll need 6 small ramekins to prepare this version that is crowned with glistening fruit gel. It's a show-stopper that would be great for a special dinner party.

1 cup sliced strawberries (store-bought berries work fine)

1 cup dark-colored wild fruit juice such as wild cherry

½ to ¾ cup sugar

2 tablespoons cold water

1½ teaspoons unflavored gelatin

Panna cotta:

2 tablespoons cold water

2 teaspoons unflavored gelatin

1 cup half-and-half

½ cup (packed) golden brown sugar

2 cups buttermilk

1 teaspoon vanilla extract

Lightly spray 6 ramekins (1 cup each) with nonstick spray. Arrange in a baking dish that holds them comfortably. Divide strawberries evenly between ramekins; set aside. In small, non-aluminum saucepan, combine juice and ½ cup sugar. Heat the mixture over medium heat, stirring constantly, until sugar dissolves. Cool slightly and taste for sweetness; add additional sugar as needed until the sweetness is the way you like it.

Pour cold water into small bowl. Sprinkle gelatin evenly over water; set aside for 5 minutes. Near the end of the 5 minutes, heat fruit juice mixture over medium-high heat until it is boiling gently. Scrape the gelatin mixture into the fruit juice, stirring vigorously to combine. Boil gently for about a minute, then remove from heat and pour into individual ramekins. Freeze until just set, about 30 minutes; or refrigerate until set, 2 to 3 hours.

When the gel is set, prepare the panna cotta: Pour cold water into small bowl. Sprinkle gelatin evenly over water; set aside for 5 minutes. In medium, non-aluminum saucepan, stir together half-and-half and brown sugar; heat over medium-high heat, stirring constantly, until sugar dissolves. Scrape the gelatin mixture into the half-and-half, stirring vigorously to combine. Remove from heat and cool to lukewarm, stirring frequently. Stir in buttermilk and vanilla. Pour over set gel; cover entire dish with plastic wrap and refrigerate until firm, about 4 hours; can be prepared up to 2 days in advance.

To serve, run a thin knife around the edge of each ramekin, then hold a ramekin in a shallow pan of very hot water for a few seconds to loosen bottom. Place an individual dessert plate over the ramekin and flip the two over as one, holding together tightly. Gently remove ramekin; repeat with remaining desserts. Serve immediately.

Wild Silk Pie with Cream Cheese Topping

1 pie (8 servings)

This pie is very sweet and rich, so a little goes a long way.

1 purchased shortbread crust or deep graham-cracker crust

1 can (14 ounces) sweetened condensed milk (reduced-fat works fine)

4 egg yolks

1 whole egg

**¾ cup wild fruit syrup, or
⅔ cup wild fruit juice mixed with ⅔ cup sugar**

2 packages (3 ounces each) cream cheese, softened

½ cup powdered sugar

½ cup sour cream (reduced-fat works fine)

1 teaspoon vanilla extract

Heat oven to 350°F. Bake the crust for 5 minutes. Remove from oven and set aside to cool while you prepare the filling. Reduce oven to 325°F.

In large mixing bowl, combine sweetened condensed milk, egg yolks, whole egg and syrup (or juice/sugar mixture). Beat with electric mixer or sturdy whisk until smooth and completely combined. Place prepared crust onto a baking sheet, and pour in the condensed-milk mixture. Bake in center of oven for about 45 minutes, or until knife inserted in center of pie comes out clean.

While pie is baking, prepare cream cheese topping: In medium mixing bowl, combine cream cheese, powdered sugar, sour cream and vanilla. Beat with electric mixer or wooden spoon until smooth and uniform. When pie filling tests done, remove pie from oven and spread cream cheese mixture evenly over the top, spreading gently with rubber spatula. Return to oven and bake for 10 to 15 minutes longer, or until cream cheese mixture can be touched lightly without sticking. Remove pie from oven and cool completely before covering and placing in refrigerator to chill for several hours. Serve cold.

Cappuccino with Flavor Shot

Just like at the expensive coffee house! You need an espresso machine to make these, but that piece of equipment is becoming quite common in the well-stocked kitchen.

1 tablespoon black cherry syrup or other wild fruit syrup per serving, or to taste

Cold, fresh milk (skim, lowfat or whole)

Finely ground espresso coffee beans

Prepare the espresso maker, getting it up to temperature and ready to steam. Pour the syrup into a large mug; set it aside while you prepare the milk and coffee. Fill the metal pitcher about half full; clip a milk thermometer inside the pitcher so its tip is just below the surface of the milk. Froth the milk with the steam wand, holding the pitcher so the wand is at an angle with the tip just under the surface of the milk. Steam to a temperature of 150°F. Set aside; the temperature will rise another 5°F while it sits.

Pack a full measure of finely ground espresso into the filter basket and tamp it firmly. Pull a shot into a shot glass or other measure, then pour into the mug; for a double, pull a second shot and add it to the mug. Immediately pour the steamed milk into the cup, holding back the froth with a spoon; fill the mug half to two-thirds full of steamed milk. Spoon the froth over the coffee, filling the mug to the brim.

 Some baristas chill the metal milk pitcher for a few minutes in the freezer to produce better froth. Also, some steam the milk first, then "pull the shot" of espresso; others make the espresso before steaming the milk.

Italian Cremosa Soda

A cooling beverage that is welcome in hot weather.

3 tablespoons raspberry syrup or other wild fruit syrup

½ cup cold whole milk, or a mix of milk and half-and-half

Crushed ice

Carbonated water

In a tall glass, stir together the syrup and milk. Fill glass half full with crushed ice; add carbonated water to the brim. Serve with a straw, and a tall spoon for mixing.

GENERAL INSTRUCTIONS and INFORMATION

The information that follows applies to a number of fruits in this book. Here you'll find information on making syrup, jelly and jam; dehydrating fruits and making fruit leathers; sterilizing canning jars; and processing in a water-bath canner.

Wild Berry or Fruit Syrup   About 1½ cups syrup per cup of juice

This works great with juice from a variety of wild berries and fruits. Use it as you would use maple syrup: on pancakes, over ice cream, on hot cereal, etc. For a refreshing beverage, pour a few tablespoons of syrup into a glass of sparkling water with ice cubes, or add a bit of syrup to a glass of chilled white wine.

1 cup juice from wild berries or fruit

Sugar as directed in Group lists below

3 tablespoons corn syrup

Group A (use 1 cup sugar per cup of juice): Apples, autumn olives, blackberries, choke-cherries, crabapples, currants, dewberries, grapes, hawthorns, mulberries, muscadines, raspberries, wild cherries.

Group B (use 1¼ cups sugar per cup of juice): Cranberries, elderberries (also add 1 teaspoon lemon juice), gooseberries, plums, prickly pears, rose hips.

Group C (use 1½ cups sugar per cup of juice): Chokeberries, highbush cranberries.

Prepare jars, bands and lids as directed on pg. 185 (even if you won't be canning the syrup, it's a good idea to sterilize the jars and lids as directed). In medium non-aluminum saucepan, combine juice and sugar. Heat over medium-high heat, stirring constantly, until sugar dissolves and mixture just begins to boil. Adjust heat so mixture boils gently. Add corn syrup and cook, stirring almost constantly, for 5 minutes; watch for boilover and adjust the heat to prevent a too-vigorous boil. After 5 minutes, pour into hot, steril-ized jars; seal with new lids and clean bands. To can, process in boiling-water bath for 10 minutes (see pg. 185 for canning instructions). Or, cool and store in the refrigerator.

The instructions are for 1 cup of prepared juice; however, you can proportionally increase the ingredients for any amount of juice.

Jelly Instructions (using pectin)

Pectin is a substance that helps fruit juices set, or jell, when making jelly or jam. Most fruits—wild or domestic—don't have enough natural pectin to set properly, so pectin needs to be added. Packaged pectin comes in two forms: a powder, typically sold in a 1.75-ounce box, and a liquid, typically sold in a box containing two 3-ounce pouches. (In the past, liquid pectin was sold in a larger bottle; the cook had to measure it out.) The packages contain helpful inserts with recipes for common domestic fruits; some of these, such as black raspberries, crabapples and currants, also grow in the wild, so you can use the recipes in the box for those fruits—if you have enough juice. Other wild fruits are not included on the insert, but those that make good jelly have been included in this book. Recipes for jelly are found throughout this book, with individual fruit accounts; the instructions below are general, and apply to all jelly recipes that use packaged pectin.

Recipes that come with packaged pectin are very specific, calling for precise amounts of fruit juice, sugar and pectin, and exact cooking procedures. However, these recipes require a lot of juice—as much as 7 cups, depending on the type of fruit. A box of powdered pectin makes more jelly—and requires more juice—than a pouch of liquid pectin. For example, a batch of currant jelly made with Sure-Jell® powdered pectin, prepared according to the recipe in the box, requires 6½ cups of juice and yields 9 cups of jelly; a batch made with Certo® liquid pectin requires 5 cups of juice and yields 8 cups of jelly.

Wild fruit juice is not always easy to come by, and you may want to use some of it for other recipes rather than making, say, 10 jars of one type of jelly. Liquid pectin allows you to make a smaller amount, but it still might use more juice than you want. Another option is to divide the pectin to make small-batch jelly; this requires a bit of tinkering.

The most challenging task is dividing the packaged pectin into smaller amounts, and it's important to measure accurately. The best method is to weigh the contents of a full box of pectin on a gram scale (ounce scales are not precise enough), then weigh out the portion you need. For example, the powder in a 1.75-ounce box of Sure-Jell® pectin I checked weighs 51 grams, so if a recipe calls for ⅔ of a box, use 34 grams (51 divided by 3 is 17; multiply by 2 to get 34). If you don't have a gram scale, measure the powder very carefully with measuring spoons (scoop or spoon the powder into the measuring spoon until it is completely full, then level off the top with the back of a knife), then divide accordingly. The same box of powdered pectin that weighs 51 grams measures 16½ teaspoons (5 tablespoons plus 1½ teaspoons) with my measuring spoons, so ⅔ of a box would be 11 teaspoons (16.5 divided by 3 is 5.5; multiply by 2 to get 11).

Small-batch jelly also cooks slightly differently than large-batch jelly, such as those on the insert in the pectin box; the smaller batch loses proportionally more liquid due to evaporation than a larger batch. If you're experimenting with your own small-batch recipes, you'll need to add just a bit more liquid than what would be indicated by simply dividing a full-batch recipe. Standard recipes also account for varying amounts of natural pectin that is in specific fruits, and so use varying amounts of juice in proportion to the added pectin depending on the type of fruit. Wild fruits vary quite a bit in natural pectin content, especially if they're not fully ripe. And some jellies take a week or even longer to set up—wild cherry is one I've had this experience with.

In summary, when working with wild fruits, you may occasionally end up with jelly that doesn't set, or jelly that is too firm. If the jelly is still liquid-like 10 days after processing, use it like syrup; it will be delicious. If the jelly is too solid, you can melt it and stir in a little water before using. Another option for too-firm jelly (or jam) is to serve it as "cheese." Set the jar in a pan of very hot water for a few minutes, then slide the jelly out onto a plate. Slice it, and serve it on its own, or use the slices to top toast that's been smeared with cream cheese. Gooseberries are often prepared as "cheese" in England and served in this fashion. It's a delicious solution for jelly or jam that is too thick to spread.

How to cook jelly with added pectin
Prepare half-pint canning jars, bands and lids as described on pg. 185. Measure the sugar you'll need, and set it aside so it is ready to use. Combine juice, and lemon juice if listed, in a non-aluminum saucepan or pot that holds at least four times the amount of juice you're using. Whisk in powdered pectin until dissolved; add butter if using (it helps reduce foaming). Heat to boiling over high heat, stirring frequently. When mixture comes to a full, rolling boil that can't be stirred down, add the sugar. Cook, stirring constantly, until the mixture again comes to a full, foaming boil. Boil for 1 minute, stirring constantly (if mixture threatens to boil over, move from heat for a few seconds, then reduce heat slightly and return pan to heat). Remove from heat, and stir for a minute or 2 to settle the foam; if there is still foam on top, skim with a clean spoon and discard. Pour into prepared jars, leaving ¼ inch headspace; seal with prepared lids and bands. Process in boiling-water bath for 10 minutes (see pg. 185), or cool and store in refrigerator.

Here are recipes for specific wild-fruit jellies (also see "Freezer jams and jellies" on pg. 181):
Apple or crabapple, pg. 7
Autumn olive, pg. 16
Blackberry or dewberry, pg. 20
Cherry and chokecherry, pg. 38
Chokeberry or aronia, pg. 46
Cranberry, pg. 50
Currant, pg. 54
Elderberry and elderberry-sumac, pgs. 61, 63
Gooseberry (ripe), pg. 65
Grape, pg. 71
Hawthorn, pg. 84
Highbush cranberry, pg. 88
Maypop, pg. 93
Mountain ash, pg. 96
Mulberry, pg. 99
Plum, pg. 134
Prickly pear, pg. 141
Raspberry (red or black) or purple-flowering raspberry, pg. 146
Rose hip and rose hip-apple, pgs. 149, 150

Jelly Instructions for Fruits with Natural Pectin

Some fruit juices, such as apple juice, have enough natural pectin that they will set without the addition of commercial pectin. However, natural pectin content varies depending on the ripeness of the fruit, time of year and other conditions, so exact cooking times can't be given; the times listed in individual recipes are a general guideline. There are three ways to test for doneness; here are directions for all three. Use whichever you prefer; you may even want to use two tests on a batch of jelly until you gain experience in jelly-making.

The temperature method is the most scientific test to judge doneness. At 8°F above the boiling point of water, the sugar concentration is high enough that the liquid should jell when it cools; once your mixture reaches that point, it's done. The temperature method works well, but it can be difficult to get a reading. Candy or deep-fat thermometers can be clipped to the side of the pan and monitored throughout cooking, but most need to be immersed into an inch (or more) of boiling liquid to read properly, and that's difficult with a small batch of jelly. Instant-read thermometers require less immersion, but they can't be left in place for more than a few minutes. You can hold them with a tongs and put the tip into the mixture, but it's steamy work because, in spite of the name, these thermometers don't really read "instantly"; it can take up to two minutes.

The temperature method also requires a bit of testing before you start cooking the jelly. We think of 212°F as the "boiling point" of water, but in fact, water boils at different temperatures depending on altitude; even at the same altitude, the boiling temperature may change from day to day depending on atmospheric conditions. Just before you make a batch of jelly, test the boiling temperature on that day, with your particular thermometer (these vary, too; if you test two at the same time, one may show boiling at 212°F, while another shows boiling at, say, 216°F). Add 8 to the boiling temperature shown on your thermometer that day, then cook your jelly to that temperature (so if your thermometer reads 213°F for a pan of boiling water, cook your jelly to 221°F).

The spoon test is also called the sheeting test. To use this method, dip a clean, cool metal spoon into the jelly kettle to spoon up a bit of the mixture. Quickly raise it a foot above the jelly kettle, out of the steam, and turn it sideways so the mixture drips back into the kettle off the side of the spoon. If the mixture forms two large drips that flow together and fall off the spoon in a sheet, it is done; get it off the heat immediately. Sometimes, your range hood gets in the way of this test; and, you need a supply of clean, cool spoons in case you need to test the jelly several times.

The cold-plate test is foolproof and easy to use, but sometimes, it's hard to know when to start testing. Many cooks use the spoon test as a preliminary, and follow up with the cold-plate test to confirm doneness. To use the cold-plate test, place a ceramic plate in the freezer to chill when you start boiling the jelly mixture. When you think the jelly is approaching doneness, drop a teaspoon of the mixture onto the cold plate and return it to the freezer for about a minute. Remove the plate from the freezer, and push at the jelly with your fingertip. If the surface wrinkles and the jelly seems firm, with no weeping around the edge, the jelly is done; get it off the heat immediately. If it is not done, return the plate to the freezer and continue cooking the jelly, testing again in a few minutes.

Jam Instructions (using pectin)

Making jam with added pectin is similar to making pectin-added jelly, but you start with puréed or crushed fruit rather than juice. For small-batch jam, you'll need to divide the pectin as instructed in the jelly instructions on pg. 178.

Prepare half-pint canning jars, bands and lids as described on pg. 185. Measure the sugar you'll need, and set it aside so it is ready to use. Combine puréed or crushed fruit, and lemon juice if listed, in a non-aluminum saucepan or pot that holds at least four times the amount of purée or crushed fruit you're using. Whisk in powdered pectin until dissolved; add butter if using (it helps reduce foaming). Heat to boiling over high heat, stirring frequently. When mixture comes to a full, rolling boil that can't be stirred down, add the sugar. Cook, stirring constantly, until the mixture again comes to a full, foaming boil. Boil for 1 minute, stirring constantly; if mixture threatens to boil over, move from heat for a few seconds, then reduce heat slightly and return pan to heat before it stops boiling. Remove from heat, and stir for a minute or 2 to settle the foam; if there is still foam on top, skim with a clean spoon and discard. Pour into prepared jars, leaving ¼ inch headspace; seal with prepared lids and bands. Process in boiling-water bath for 10 minutes (see pg. 185), or cool and store in refrigerator.

Here are recipes for specific wild-fruit jams using pectin:
Autumn olive, pg. 16
Blackberry, pg. 23

Freezer jams and jellies are made with added pectin, but the fruit itself is not cooked; only the pectin mixture is. Jams and jellies made in this way have a brighter, fresher flavor than those made with cooked fruit. Freezer jams and jellies are so named because jars aren't processed in a boiling-water bath; rather, they are stored in the freezer for up to a year (or in the refrigerator, where they will keep for several weeks). Instructions are included with each recipe.

Here are recipes for specific freezer jams and jellies made with wild fruits:
Blackberry jam, pg. 22
Grape jelly, pg. 71
Lower-sugar muscadine jelly, pg. 111
Serviceberry or blueberry jam, pg. 154
Strawberry jam, pg. 162

Dehydrating Wild Berries and Fruits

Home drying, or dehydrating, is an excellent preservation method for many wild fruits. It works on a simple principle: Warm air is circulated over prepared foods to remove the moisture. Food is held on a tray that allows maximum air flow. Several home dehydrators are available; your oven can also be used. Dehydrators come with their own trays. For oven dehydrating, stretch a piece of bridal-veil netting over a cake-cooling rack, then secure it with twist-ties. Fruit leathers need to be dried on a solid liner sheet (dehydrator) or plastic-lined baking sheet (oven); see pg. 184 for information on fruit leathers.

Fruits can generally be dried with no preparation other than washing and perhaps slicing. (In comparison, vegetables generally need to be blanched, or par-boiled, before dehydrating.) As a general rule, if a fruit can be frozen with no special preparation, it can also be dried with no special preparation. Some fruits dehydrate better if they are first syrup-blanched; the dried fruit will be softer and stickier than untreated fruit, and will have more vibrant color. To prepare the syrup, combine 1 cup sugar and 1 cup white corn syrup with 2 cups water. Heat to boiling, stirring until sugar dissolves. Add fruit; reduce heat and simmer for 5 minutes. Drain and rinse fruit in cold water before drying.

Arrange foods on the trays in even layers, ideally with air space between each piece. However, keep in mind that the food will shrink as it dries, so the spaces between the foods will grow. Stir, turn over or rearrange the food periodically during drying, to separate pieces that may be stuck together and to promote even drying.

Quality home dehydrators have thermostats; 145°F works well for fruits. If you're drying in the oven, set it to the lowest setting, and prop the door slightly ajar with a ball of foil or an empty can; this allows moisture to escape, and also keeps the temperature down.

To check foods for dryness, remove a piece or two from the dehydrator or oven, and cool to room temperature before judging doneness. (If you're making fruit leather, remove the entire tray and let it cool slightly before checking.) Some individual pieces may be dry sooner than others; simply remove them from the trays and continue drying the rest until everything is finished. Let the food stand at room temperature for an hour or so, then pack into clean glass jars, seal tightly and store in a cool, dark location. Check it several times over the next few days to be sure that moisture isn't developing inside the jars; if you see any moisture, take the food out and dry it some more in the dehydrator or oven. Properly dehydrated foods retain their quality and freshness for a year or longer. If you notice any mold, however, discard the entire contents of the jar without tasting; moisture has gotten in somehow and compromised the food, and it is no longer safe.

Note: The information here comes largely from my books, *Abundantly Wild: Collecting and Cooking Wild Edibles in the Upper Midwest*, and *The Back-Country Kitchen: Camp Cooking for Canoeists, Hikers and Anglers*.

Blueberries: Frozen or fresh blueberries both dry well, and require no pretreatment; fresh blueberries can be dipped briefly into boiling water to "check" (break) the skin, which reduces drying time. Doneness test: Hard, dark, wrinkled; frozen and "checked" blueberries will be slightly flattened when dry. Drying time: 6 to 8 hours.

Crabapple wedges: Crabapples can be dried with no additional preparation, or syrup-blanched first. To prepare either blanched or unblanched crabapples, quarter washed fruit, removing seeds and blossom end. Syrup-blanch for 5 minutes if you like. Doneness test: The blanched crabapples will be glossy and slightly sticky, with dark-red peels and pinkish flesh; they are rather like a leathery candy. Unblanched crabapples are dry and leathery and have a duller appearance, with tan flesh and brick-red skins. Drying time: 4 to 5½ hours, depending on size of crabapples.

Cranberries: Frozen or fresh cranberries both dry well; those which have been frozen dry a bit more quickly. Blanch in boiling water for about a minute, or until the skins split. Drain and allow to dry before spreading on racks. Doneness test: Shrunken, wrinkled, leathery, dark red. Drying time: 6 to 10 hours.

Currants or gooseberries: Frozen or fresh berries both dry well, and require no pre-treatment; fresh berries can be dipped briefly into boiling water to "check" (break) the skin, which reduces drying time. Don't dry prickly gooseberries; the prickles become stiffer, making them very unpleasant to eat. Doneness test: Hard, dark, wrinkled; frozen and "checked" berries will be slightly flattened when dry. Drying time: 8 to 10 hours.

Elderberries: Spread washed elderberries (stemlets removed) on mesh liners over drying trays (elderberries get quite small when dried, and will fall through normal dryer trays). Doneness test: Shrunken and hard. Drying time: 4 to 5 hours.

Ground cherries: Frozen or fresh ground cherries both dry well. Wash and cut into halves; arrange, cut-side up, on dryer trays. Doneness test: They will shrink and flatten quite a bit, becoming leathery; color will deepen. Drying time: About 5 hours.

Mountain ash berries: These mealy berries dry well at room temperature; simply spread them on baking sheets and let stand at room temperature until dry, stirring several times a day. To hasten drying, spread individual berries, or even small berry clusters, on the tray of a food dehydrator or baking sheet for oven drying. Doneness test: Leathery and hard, deep brick color. Drying time (dehydrator or oven): 3 to 4 hours.

Mulberries or raspberries: Spread in single layer on solid liner sheets or baking sheets (for oven drying) to catch drips; no pretreatment is needed. If you like, transfer fruits to regular (ventilated) dryer trays after an hour or 2, after any juices have been released, to hasten drying. Doneness test: Leathery and shrunken. Drying time: 4 to 10 hours; raspberries dry more quickly than mulberries.

Muscadines: Halve, remove seeds and skin as directed on pg. 104. Spread in single layer on dryer trays that have been sprayed with nonstick spray. Doneness test: Shrunken and flat, leathery. Drying time: 7½ to 9 hours. Refrigerate to prevent them sticking together.

Persimmons: For *underripe* persimmons (slightly soft): Peel with swivel-bladed peeler, then cut ¼ inch thick and remove seeds; arrange in single layer on dryer trays. For *ripe* persimmons: Cut in half, scoop out flesh with teaspoon and remove seeds; place on liner sheets. Doneness test: Slices from underripe fruit will be leathery and pliable, with no sticky spots; the ripe fruit slices will be like a raisin, but should not be wet or overly sticky. Drying time: 4½ to 6 hours for underripe sliced fruits, 5 to 8 hours for ripe fruits.

Plums: Halve plums and remove pits. Plums can be dried with no further pretreatment, or syrup-blanched first. Arrange plum halves, blanched or not, cut-side up, on dryer trays. Doneness test: Shrunken, firm and leathery; blanched plums will be softer and stickier when dry, while untreated fruit will be harder and more chewy. Drying time: 8 to 24 hours, depending on size of fruit.

Serviceberries: Remove stem and blossom ends. Cut fruits in half for quicker drying, or dry whole. Arrange in single layer on trays. Doneness test: Shrunken and leathery. Drying time: 6 to 10 hours.

Strawberries: Wash; remove cap. Arrange on trays no more than 2 deep. Doneness test: Leathery and somewhat spongy. Drying time: 4 to 8 hours, depending on size.

Wild Berry or Fruit Leather

Most fruits can be dried into a leather; generally, all you need to do is simply purée the fruit in a blender or food processor, sweeten to taste as needed, and dry in a food dehydrator or low oven. (Please read the general information on dehydrating foods on pg. 182.) Hard fruits, such as apples and pears, should be cooked in a little water with a few drops of lemon juice before puréeing; soft berries can be puréed and dried with no cooking.

The purée to be dried into a leather should be fairly thick—a consistency like applesauce works well. If you try to dry a purée that is too thin or watery, the leather will take forever to dry, and may be brittle once dry. If the fruit you're working with is watery, or the purée too runny, cook it down for a bit to thicken it before spreading on the drying sheets.

You can add spices to your purées to vary the flavor; try cinnamon or nutmeg with apple or plum purée, or a bit of orange extract with berry purée. For additional interest, sprinkle the purée before drying with finely chopped nuts, shredded coconut or granola.

Commercial dryers come with solid liner sheets that work well, but I've found that some of them need to be sprayed with nonstick spray, especially if the fruit is extremely sticky. Experiment with a small batch of purée to see how your liner sheets perform. If you're drying in the oven or in a homemade dryer, line rimmed baking sheets with plastic wrap, then tape the wrap to the rims of the baking sheets to keep it in place during filling and drying. One standard-sized sheet will hold about 2 cups of purée.

Pour the purée onto prepared baking sheets or dehydrator liners. Tilt the sheets to evenly distribute the purée; it should be about ¼ inch deep. Dry at 130°-150°F until leathery with no sticky spots; peel from the sheets and flip once during drying if the bottom is not drying properly. Total drying time is generally 4 to 10 hours, but this may vary depending on your equipment, the purée and the weather. If you've used baking sheets lined with plastic wrap, the leather can be peeled off any time; if you've used solid liner sheets with a dehydrator, peel off the leather while it is still warm. Roll up all leathers, and wrap in plastic wrap. They keep well at cool room temperature if properly dried; for long-term storage, wrap the plastic-wrapped rolls in freezer wrap and store in the freezer.

Sterilizing Jars and Canning

Jars and lids used for canning need to be sterilized before filling. It's also a good idea to sterilize jars for jams and jellies even if you plan to store the finished product in the refrigerator or freezer. Modern canning jars have two-piece tops: a flat lid, and a screw-on band. When you're canning, always start with a brand-new lid; the rubber seal won't work if the lid has been used before. Bands can be re-used a number of times, but if they start to get corroded, get rid of them and buy new bands.

Always use jars specially made for canning. These jars can be re-used many times, unless they develop a nick or crack. Inspect each jar by holding it up to the light, looking for cracks or fractures. Then, when you are washing the jar prior to sterilizing it, run your wet finger over the top rim of the jar, checking for nicks. Even a small nick will cause canning failure; if you find jars like this in your collection, pack them up for recycling.

The recipes in this book call for half-pint jars. These are small enough to fit in a large pot such as a Dutch oven, so you don't have to use a full-sized water bath canner. The jars shouldn't sit directly on the bottom of the pot because they might crack from the heat. If you have a rack or a pasta-cooking insert for your pot, use that to raise the jars above the bottom; otherwise, line the bottom of the pot with a clean, thick towel.

Jelly and jam should be poured into the jars the minute they are done cooking, so the jars must be sterilized and ready to go before you start cooking. Wash jars, bands and lids in hot, soapy water, inspecting the rim; rinse well. Place jars on the rack in the pot, then add water to cover them by an inch. Heat to boiling over high heat. Boil the jars for 10 minutes, then turn off the heat and let the jars sit in the hot water until you're ready to fill them. Meanwhile, place washed lids and bands in a saucepan; cover with water. Heat to a vigorous simmer. Cover and remove from heat.

When the jelly or jam is ready, use canning tongs to remove one jar from the pot, pouring its water back into the pot. Fill the jar with food, leaving the amount of head space indicated in the recipe ("head space" is the empty area at the top of the jar). Wipe the jar rim and threads with a clean paper towel. Place a hot lid and band on top, and screw the band on so it is just finger-tight. If you will be canning the food, return the jar to the pot and repeat with remaining food; otherwise, place the filled jar on a rack to cool.

How to process food in a hot-water bath

Once the jars are filled and returned to the pot, add additional hot water if necessary to cover the jars by 1 inch. Heat to boiling over high heat, then begin timing and boil for the amount of time indicated in the recipe. Use canning tongs to remove the jars from the pot, grasping them below the bands (if you grasp the band itself, you could break the seal). Place jars on a thick towel, away from drafts, to cool. When cool, check each jar for a proper seal. The center of the lid should be depressed, and it should not move up and down when pressed with a finger. If any jars are improperly sealed, refrigerate and enjoy as you would any opened jelly or jam. Sealed jars can be stored in a cool, dark place for up to a year.

BIBLIOGRAPHY

Bittman, Mark. *How to Cook Everything*. New York, NY: Macmillan, a Simon & Schuster Macmillan Company, 1998.

Brill, Steven. *Identifying and Harvesting Edible and Medicinal Plants in Wild (and Not So Wild) Places*. New York, NY: William Morrow, an imprint of HarperCollins Publishers Inc., 1994.

Corriher, Shirley O. *CookWise: The Hows & Whys of Successful Cooking*. New York, NY: William Morrow and Company, Inc., 1997.

Derig, Betty B. and Fuller, Margaret C. *Wild Berries of the West*. Missoula, MT: Mountain Press Publishing Company, 2001.

Gibbons, Euell. *Stalking the Wild Asparagus*. New York, NY: David McKay Company, Inc., 1962.

Hibler, Janie. *The Berry Bible*. New York, NY: William Morrow, an imprint of HarperCollins Publishers Inc., 2004.

Liddell, Caroline and Weir, Robin. *Frozen Desserts*. New York, NY: St. Martin's Griffin, 1996.

Lyle, Katie Letcher. *The Wild Berry Book: Romance, Recipes and Remedies*. Minnetonka, MN: NorthWord Press, 1994.

Marrone, Teresa. *Abundantly Wild: Collecting and Cooking Wild Edibles in the Upper Midwest* and *The Seasonal Cabin Cookbook*. Cambridge, MN: Adventure Publications, Inc., 2004 and 2001.

Marrone, Teresa. *The Back-Country Kitchen: Camp Cooking for Canoeists, Hikers and Anglers*. Minneapolis, MN: Northern Trails Press, 1996.

Peterson, Lee Allen. *A Field Guide to Edible Wild Plants of Eastern and Central North America*. Boston, MA: Houghton Mifflin Company, 1977.

Thayer, Samuel. *The Forager's Harvest* and *Nature's Garden*. Birchwood, WI: Forager's Harvest, 2006 and 2010.

U.S. Department of Agriculture, USDA National Nutrient Database for Standard Reference, Release 21 (http://www.ars.usda.gov/nutrientdata).

Young, Kay. *Wild Seasons: Gathering and Cooking Wild Plants of the Great Plains*. Lincoln, NE: University of Nebraska Press, 1993.

INDEX

ABOUT THE AUTHOR

Teresa Marrone has been gathering and preparing wild edibles for more than 20 years. She was formerly Managing Editor of a series of outdoors-themed cookbooks and other books, and is the author of *Abundantly Wild: Collecting and Cooking Wild Edibles in the Upper Midwest*, as well as numerous outdoors-related cookbooks. Teresa also writes magazine articles on wild foods and cooking. *Cooking with Wild Berries & Fruits of Indiana, Kentucky and Ohio* combines her various skills and interests into a clear, concise, easy-to-use book that helps the user appreciate the diversity of the various wild berries and fruits that grow in this region. Teresa lives in Minneapolis with husband Bruce and their Senegal parrot, Tuca.